Magic Man
The Life and Films of Steven Spielberg

by

William Schoell

Tudor Publishers
Greensboro

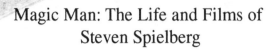

Magic Man: The Life and Films of
Steven Spielberg

Printed in the United States of America

First Edition

Library of Congress Cataloging-in-Publication Data

Schoell, William.
    Magic man: the life and films of Steven Spielberg/ by William Schoel. — 1st ed.
    P.   cm.
    Includes bibliographical references and index.
    Summary: A biography of the motion picture producer and director Steven Spielberg, with an emphasis on the events in his life that have found expression in his films.
    ISBN 0-936389-57-5
    1. Spielberg, Steven, 1947-   –Juvenile literature. 2. Motion picture producers and directors—United States—Biography—Juvenile literature. [1. Spielberg, Steven, 1947—   . 2. Motion picture producers and directors.]   I. Title.
PN1998.3.S65S36   1998
891.43'02330092—dc21   97-40181
[B]   CIP
                                                                                  AC

Contents

Acknowledgments

Many thanks to Universal Studios; Zanuck/Brown Productions; Paramount Studios; George Lucas Productions; Steven Spielberg Productions; Amblin Entertainment, Inc.; Lucasfilm Ltd.; Gulf and Western; Warner Brothers; and all those involved in the making of Steven Spielberg's films.

The photographs contained in this book are from the author's private collection.

To My Parents

Chapter 1

8mm Genius

When he was five years old, Steven Spielberg's parents took him to see his first movie, *The Greatest Show on Earth*. As he sat wide-eyed in the audience, little Steven was convinced that the actors and animals up on the giant screen were going to "get out at him," although his father assured him that was not possible. Steven wondered when the cast of the picture would be joining him in the audience, or when an elephant might barrel off the screen and up the aisle.

Steven was apprehensive, but he was also awed. He wanted to be a part of the excitement. If the people in the movie couldn't come down to him, perhaps he could be pulled up into the screen with them. Years later he would have an opportunity to do just that, if only in a figurative sense. His lifelong fascination with the cinema had begun.

Steven was born on December 18th, 1946, in Ohio. His father, Arnold Spielberg, was an electrical engineer, and later, a computer expert. His mother, Leah, had been a concert pianist. Steven's practical and technical side was inherited from his father, while his artistic side, his creative vision, came from his mother.

To hear him tell it, Spielberg was a nerdy kid with few friends and hardly any social skills. He has told many interviewers about how he was picked on by neighorhood bullies and made fun of at school. Being Jewish, he was also the victim of anti-Semitic jibes, as he lived in a primarily Gentile community.

But some of his relatives remember a different story, that even as a boy Steven exhibited the forceful nature that would serve him well when he became a film director years later. He won over the bullies and made friends easily.

When Steven was twelve, his father got an 8mm movie camera (which used film eight millimeters wide instead of the videotape used in today's camcorders). Steven convinced his father to let him photograph all of the family outings and birthday parties, and before long had the camera for his personal use.

Steven had a set of Lionel model trains which he loved to crash over and over again, with the result that many of the cars would break and his father would have to replace them. Arnold Spielberg told Steven if he broke another train, he'd take the set away from him. Steven decided to use the 8mm camera to film the train wreck. That way he'd always have a record of it. Looking at the film he made, according to Spielberg, "satisfied my urge to wreck my trains."

The little movie of the train wreck looked surprisingly good. By then, Steven had already developed certain cinematic instincts. He placed the camera below the trains and shot upward, so that when the film was projected the cars looked much larger than they were; almost real, in fact.

From then on there was no stopping Steven. He got everyone into the act. Arnold built sets for his 8mm masterpieces. Leah sent notes to the school saying Steven was "sick" when he really wasn't, just so he could stay home to go out on "location" or edit one of the movies. His three sisters and several classmates were drafted as cast members.

On some occasions, Leah, would even appear in a film, as when she tore around Camelback Mountain in a jeep, wearing a helmet, in a weird mini-war flick. In this epic, which Steven named *Escape to Nowhere*, he filmed a World War II battle in the desert. He cast a school bully as the hero (one way to get him to stop picking on him) and used huge puffs of ordinary flour to simulate explosions. It won a local childrens' home movie contest.

Steven delighted in casting his sisters in horror films, and terrifying them in general. He'd tell them spooky stories, lock them in closets, rig up lighted plastic skulls in their bedroom, timing it so that the skull would start to glow when they turned the lights out. If something really got them to scream, he'd use it in a movie.

Steven became so obsessed with his movies that he neglected everything else. His room was so filthy that his mother shuddered in horror each time she opened the door. He kept lizards, parakeets and other animals in his room, all of whom were allowed to roam free and use any spot they chose as a personal toilet. His mother swore that she could see things growing under his bed.

His school work suffered, and his grades were terrible. In the Boy Scouts he failed to get most of his merit badges because he was inept at almost everything. He did earn a photography badge, however, by turning in an 8mm film instead of still pictures. "Gunsmore" was a three-minute spoof of the TV western "Gunsmoke," which featured gunfights, stagecoach robberies, and everything else Steven had seen on TV.

Steven didn't get much inspiration from books. Sad to say, he got little pleasure out of reading. He became obsessed with films so early that the joy and importance of reading was never ignited in him. Some critics argue that most of his films remain distinctly shallow and juvenile—influenced by television and pop culture and old movies instead of genuinely original—because of this. Steven had some interest in music, joining the school band and playing an adequate clarinet. And he was a bona-fide entrepreneur at a very early age.

Steven would charge money for kids in the neighborhood to see his and other 8mm films at his house. Members of the audience also had to pay for popcorn, soda, and other snacks. He also put on puppet shows and charged admission for them. And he developed enough confidence to enter hospitals and ask them if he could shoot some footage in the emergency rooms! One time he took his cast to a local airport and asked them to close down one of the runways for a few minutes so he could shoot an important sequence. Amazingly, none of the officials ever said no to Steven Spielberg.

When Steven was in high school, he made his first full-length movie, a two-and-a-half-hour science fiction film entitled *Firelight*. In this film, scientists (whatever adults he could enlist) investigate "firelights" in the sky that turn out to be Unidentified Flying Objects. His sisters were ordinary citizens who spot the firelight from their backyard. Out of the UFO come "things with jaws (that) gobble up everything in sight," as Spielberg described it years later. *Firelight* was a crude—and much more sinister—version of *Close Encounters of the Third Kind.*

Steven talked a local movie theater into "premiering" the film on a slow night. Naturally, he charged admission. He managed to make enough to pay for the film, which cost $400 to make. A far cry from the many millions his films would cost years later.

Chapter 2

Boy Wonder

It was a terrible blow to Steven when his parents separated when he was sixteen; a divorce soon followed. The marriage had always been filled with tension, and Steven would console his sisters when they heard their parents arguing. Perhaps in an effort to avoid dealing with his painful private life, Steven emersed himself even more in films and fantasy.

After graduating high school, Steven tried to enroll in the UCLA film school, but his grades were too poor. He wound up instead at California State University at Long Beach, where he made several surrealistic student films that were nothing like the ones he'd directed years later. Budget constrictions and a lack of strong actors led him, like many student filmmakers before and after, to make "weird" pictures that were weak on plot line.

For instance, there was the one about a man who is being chased around campus by someone who wants to kill him. The protagonist is so caught up in the enjoyment of running, that he doesn't remember who is after him or why. Another was a study of rain hitting earth and turning into mud, which didn't even require actors.

Steven had little interest in the politcial events going on in the nation at the time (protests against the Vietnam war for one thing); he was only focused on becoming a filmmaker. He decided that one of his movies had to be a more "serious" effort, or at least would not look like a "kid" movie if he showed it to a studio. And he had good reason to believe that he might be able to get studio execs to look at one of his movies.

When he began attending Cal State, Steven often sneaked out of school to roam around the back lots of nearby Universal Studios. "I was on the tour and jumped off the bus when no one was looking," he once said. He noticed that everyone who belonged on the lot, aside from workmen and actors, was dressed in a suit and tie, so he put on the suit he wore for his bar mitzvah and borrowed his father's briefcase. He looked just like a junior executive. This way he no longer had to sneak off the bus—he could bluff his way past the studio guard.

At first, Steven wandered around wide-eyed, watching them shoot TV shows, which by now comprised most of Universal's output. Then he became more bold, claiming an empty office and even putting his name up in the building directory. He left his name and extension number at the main switchboard! He spent more time at Universal than he did at Cal State.

When he wasn't watching them film a program, absorbing all he could about the filmmaking process, he was showing his 8mm shorts to anyone nice enough to look at them. Many of these early contacts took pity on Steven, because he seemed so anxious and, in appearance at least, totally geeky. The Universal film librarian watched some of the shorts and was impressed with them. This came in very handy when Steven completed his first mini-epic.

The epic was entitled *Amblin.'* Steven received $15,000 from a college buddy who wanted to become a producer, and asked two attractive fellow students to star in the film. *Amblin'* has no real plot; it only shows a young man and woman hitchhiking in the desert on their way to the Pacific Ocean. But the film was the first one Steven shot in more expensive and more professional 16mm, had a very "mod" look to it, which Steven later likened to a Pepsi commercial or rock video. It did not look like a hokey, amateurish student production.

Steven wanted the 22-minute film to get him attention, and it worked. He entered it in numerous film contests, and it won prizes in the Atlanta and Venice film festivals. Best of all, it really impressed the Universal film librarian who, without warning, showed it to Sid Sheinberg, head of production of Universal's television division.

On the basis of *Amblin,'* Sheinberg offered Spielberg a contract. Steven told him it was important that he get a directorial assignment by the time he was twenty-one. He did.

Sheinberg saw that Steven had talent and ability—not to mention chutzpah—and decided to use him when he needed a director for a segment of a TV pilot movie for a new series. Rod Serling, creator of *Twilight Zone*, was going to host a new show of the macabre entitled *Night Gallery*. Each story would be inspired by a painting in the gallery from where Serling would address the television audience.

Steven's work, the second of three, concerned a wealthy blind woman who pays a pathetic fellow $9000 (which he owes a loan shark) for his eyes. A new operation will allow the heartless woman to be able to see for several hours. But her plans go awry when her hours of vision coincide with a New York City blackout. The sun comes up just as her sight begins to fade. She moves forward in anger and winds up falling out a window of her penthouse.

The blind woman was played by sixty-five-year-old actress Joan Crawford, who had been a major Hollywood star before Steven had been born. "It's not like Joan Crawford was too happy with the idea of this kid directing her," said Spielberg. In fact, Crawford was appalled at his youth and inexperience and tried to get him fired, but Serling went to bat for Steven and he stayed. Once she got used to the idea of being directed by a "kid," Crawford wound up admiring the strange, intense young man who was her director.

This segment of *Night Gallery* isn't very logical, but Crawford is good and Steven tried his best to inject some cinematic élan into the proceedings. As Crawford screams out the things she plans to see after the operation—"trees, colors!"—Steven cuts closer and closer to her almost manical face. One interesting split-screen shot shows the woman's eyes directly beneath those of the poverty-stricken donor (Tom Bosley).

But Steven didn't handle everything as well as he could have, and the producer was forced to reshoot some of the scenes. In the finished product, the lack of a shot of Crawford falling to her death makes the segment end much too abruptly and inconclusively. Still, *Night Gallery* was enough to get Steven assignments directing at least one further *Night Gallery* episode (when the pilot became a weekly series), as well as episodes of the medical dramas *Marcus Welby, M. D.* and *The Spychiatrist*, and the dramatic series *The Name of the Game*.

But it was a year-and-a-half before any of these assignments materialized and Steven was getting frantic. He decided to try and speed up the process by working on story treatments and screenplays which he submitted to producers. He hoped they would buy the script and let him direct it himself. All that came out of this was the sale of a story that eventually made it to the screen as *Ace Eli and Roger of the Skies* (1973), about stunt flyers in the 1920s.

Spielberg's second TV movie, *Duel* (1971) was based on a short story by Richard Matheson, who wrote the script for the telefilm. Steven was passed a copy of the script from a mail room buddy who knew that this was just the project he was looking for. He hunted down the picture's producer and nagged and nagged at him until the producer said he could do it. When he wanted to be, Steven could be very demanding, persuasive, and persistent.

In the telefilm, a man (Dennis Weaver) driving

on the highway passes a diesel truck, which apparently angers the psychotic driver. What ensues is a chilling cat-and-mouse game in which the truck driver keeps pumping up his attack of nerves on the man in the car. By the time the movie is halfway over, the trucker has escalated to trying to kill Weaver any way he can, the highway becoming a battlefield.

Duel is frightening because the situation is so possible. The huge truck with its unseeen, malevolent driver becomes a highly plausible monster. At the end of the film, Weaver outwits his opponent by driving at the truck and diving out of his car at the last second. Ablaze, truck and driver fall over a convenient cliff.

Although there are moments in the movie when the protagonist's actions seem out of character, Spielberg's direction is on the money. *Duel* is consistently harrowing and exciting, and Weaver offers a convincing portrait of an ordinary man at the end of his rope. John A. Marta's cinematography of sweeping highways, desert vistas, and roadside shacks and diners is excellent.

The studio was so pleased with *Duel* that they released it as a theatrical feaure in Europe. The movie's success inspired other killer vehicle movies:*The Car, Crash,* and even Stephen King's

Christine. In all of these the truck and driver were replaced, respectively, by an automobile and a demonic presence. None were as effective as the more down-to-earth yet much more chilling *Duel.* The film won several European film awards, and Marta received an Emmy for Best Sound Editing).

Steven's next full-length TV thriller was quite disappointing in comparision to *Duel.* In *Something Evil* (1972), a family moves from the crime-ridden big city to a bucolic country home, only to have their little boy possessed by a demon that makes the drug dealers and gang leaders back home seem tame in comparision. Spielberg's direction was too self-conscious and "arty" to be effective this time around, and the story—a bad imitation of *The Exorcist*—never got off the ground. The cast tried their best, but couldn't prevent *Something Evil* from being more boring than scary.

Now this telefilm is all but forgotten, eclipsed not only by Steven's subsequent movies, but by one he later produced which had similarities to it: *Poltergeist.* One good thing Spielberg took away from the picture was cinematographer Bill Butler, who would later do the same honors on *Jaws.*

Speilberg followed *Somthing Evil* with another telefilm,*Savage,* which sounded like a horror-thriller but was actually a pilot for a series about investigative reporters.Two stars of the original *Mission: Impossible* series, Martin Landau and Barbara Bain, were hoping lightning would strike twice, but the TV movie did nothing for anyone's career.

One day, Steven was reading a news story about a couple who were pursued by dozens of cops when they tried to retrieve their child from a foster home, and thought it would make a good movie. He wrote a script and gave it to the producing team of Richard Zanuck and David Brown, who had bought the *Ace Eli* story. They bought this new script, called *The Sugarland Express*, and agreed to let him direct it. But they insisted upon bringing in more experienced writers to do revisions. Speilberg was so happy to be directing his first theatrical film (*Duel* didn't count as it had only been on TV in America) that he didn't protest as much as he might have otherwise.

By this time the world-wide grosses for *Duel* had been counted and added up to $9 million—for a made-for-TV movie. Zanuck and Brown might have balked at letting Speilberg helm *Sugarland* if *Duel* hadn't done as well as it had.

In the movie, a young mother (Goldie Hawn) talks her incarcerated husband (William Atherton) into breaking out of prision so he can help her get their baby back. They force a cop to come along with them on their journey to Sugarland, Texas, but along the way they are joined by dozens of highway patrolmen who are determined to stop them. Hearing of their plight, people in the towns they pass through line up through the streets to cheer the couple on.

Spielberg's believed the police had overreacted to the young couple's actions, whose crimes were comparatively petty. In this he may have been oversimlifying matters, making the characters more likable and less dangerous, than they may have been in real life. *Sugarland Express* was made in the seventies, when there was a lot of anti-police, anti-authority feeling in the country. Anyone that breaks out of prison and holds a cop hostage, despite the reason, is not going to be treated lightly.

Spielberg spent a great deal of time working with Goldie Hawn, who had starred in a silly sixties TV comedy show called *Laugh-In* , and at first could not play the part as seriously as it often needed to be. He did many takes with her until she dropped some of the ditzy, inappropriate mannerisms that had been her trademark. It was a delicate task. He couldn't risk offending her, because without her the financing for the film would collapse. The result was an excellent performance.

Spielberg's slick direction was the main selling point of the film, which garnered him and the picture terrific reviews. He was not just a TV *wunderkind* anymore; he was a legitimate theatrical movie director who had impressed some of the toughest critics in the business.

There was just one problem. *The Sugarland Express* did not make any money.

Steven needed a new, more commercial project fast.

Chapter 3

Killer Shark

Although *The Sugarland Express* did not make money, the largely positive critical notices convinced its producers, the team of Richard Zanuck and David Brown, that Spielberg was not someone to give up on. His next project with them was the one that would really put him on the map.

Zanuck and Brown had received pre-publication galleys of a book about a Great White shark terrorizing a coastal community. Written by Peter Benchley, the son of the better-known author Nathaniel Benchley, it had been heavily worked on and restructured by an editorial committee that had faith in its storyline. They felt that it could not only be a blockbuster novel, but would also make a terrific, top-grossing motion picture.

The book, of course, was *Jaws*.

Zanuck and Brown read the galleys, liked it, and made a bid for the film rights. They paid $175,000 for them. Had they waited until *Jaws* hit the bestseller lists, they would have had to pay a lot more. The publishers figured it was worth getting much less money for the rights because the publicity generated by the film version would help push the book onto the bestseller list. The book might not have made it on its own.

One afternoon, Spielberg came into Zanuck-Brown's production offices to talk and see if there were any more assignments coming his way. He spotted a copy of the *Jaws* galleys on the desk, stuck it into his pocket when no one was looking, and absently thumbed through them at home. Spielberg had never been a big reader, but he was intrigued enough by the storyline to read large sections of the book, particularly the scary portions involving the shark.

Jaws had an exciting premise, but the writing was perfunctory and the whole novel second-rate. Like many people, Steven liked the story, but was cool to the book's "romantic" subplot. This had the police chief's wife becoming involved with the oceanologist who comes to help capture the shark. He saw enough in the novel's cinematic possibilities, however, to ask the produces if he could direct the film adaptation.

Brown and Zanuck had assigned a director to *Jaws*, a much more experienced helmsman named

Dick Richards. But they sensed that Spielberg was more suited to the material, or were totally overwhelmed by his enthusiasm; soon Richards was out and Spielberg was in.

Steven told the producers that the subplot had to go, and even told the author what he thought of it. Benchley wasn't thrilled with the criticism, but he worked on three successive screenplays before throwing up his hands and moving on to another novel.

A Pulitzer-winning playwright named Howard Sackler (*The Great White Hope*) was brought in, but Steven lost patience with him when he returned the romantic subplot to the screenplay.

Finally, a writer named Carl Gottlieb—an old college friend of Steven's—was hired and the results were more felicitous.

The first thing to do was to decide where *Jaws* could be filmed. The novel took place on Long Island, but the screenplay moved the location to a smaller area, the fictional "Amity Island." The producers determined that Martha's Vineyard off Cape Cod would be the perfect.

Next came casting. Since the shark was the star, the actors could be relative unknowns. Roy Scheider was cast as police chief Brody. Richard Dreyfuss (who had previously starred in one "small" picture,

The Apprenticeship of Duddy Kravits and the well-received ensemble production, *American Graffiti*, was cast as Hooper, the oceanologist. Completely inexperienced Lorraine Gary got the role of Brody's wife. Gary was cast as a favor to Speilberg's old mentor, Sid Sheinberg; she was Sheinberg's wife.

Spielberg did not enjoy making *Jaws*. The crew were "old duffers" who were used to working with highly experienced men their own age or older; Steven was only twenty-six years old. To make matters worse, he looked seventeen. "I still had acne, and that doesn't help instill confidence in seasoned crews," he once acknowledged.

Later, Speilberg would nervously joke about how much he was hated by the crew, who saw him as "a kind of Captain Bligh." Determined to make the best picture he possibly could, and knowing how much was riding on its success, Steven made sure the crew worked as hard and as long as was necessary. He probably overcompensated for the fact that his baby face and relative inexperience did not inspire respect or confidence in the men. Therefore, he overdid the "authority" bit.

By the time the filming was over, Spielberg almost believed the rumor flying around the set: that the crew members were planning to hold him under the water until he drowned and make his death look accidental. Whatever the case, Steven left Martha's Vineyard in the night by ferry without saying goodbye to anyone involved in the production.

Steven also had problems with both the weather and the local inhabitants. Usually, filming begins early in the morning, but shooting on *Jaws* was frequently delayed until 4:00 p.m. because of sudden, unexpected squalls that brought clouds and stirred up the water. There were only two hours of good daylight for filming. Spielberg hated being on water in the first place, and the storms only made it worse.

On land, there were problems with residents who had come to Martha's Vineyard for peace, quiet, and privacy. They were infuriated at seeing messy-looking crew members with blaring radios everywhere they turned. The *Jaws* cast and crew must have seemed like a veritable invasion to them. They retaliated by making noise during land-based shots or by deliberately walking into camera range and necessitating a second—or twentieth—take.

The townspeople also proved how prickly they could be when Steven sent out word that he needed some smaller sharks, which he hoped they could supply. This was for the scene when some Amity Island fishermen display a shark that they wrongly

believe is responsible for the carnage. Several
fishermen promised to deliver a few likely con-
tenders before the scene was scheduled to be shot,
but when the time came, there was nary a shark—
or fisherman—in sight. Spielberg finally got a dead
Tiger shark shipped from Florida which stank up
the dock waitng for its close up. Suddenly, dozens
of dead sharks were thrown onto the pier where the
producers had set up headquarters. "Where were
these sharks when I needed them?" Spielberg
wondered.

All these delays meant that the picture started
going over budget and over schedule. Brown and
Zanuck had a meeting with Spielberg and told him
that either things got cooking or they would have
to find a new director. Upset and worried, Steven
took out his anxiety on the crew, only making them
more resentful. He also argued with the producers
about the "casting" of the shark.

Brown and Zanuck felt that real Great Whites
should be used in the picture. Waiting for the
mechanical stand-in that was being constructed at
Steven's urging was too costly and time-consuming.
Steven argued Great Whites could not be trained
as if they were seals or dophins. He agreed to hire
some documentarians to take footage of real Great
Whites, however. The experts adamantly backed him

up and told the producers that sharks could not live in captivity. The idea of capturing one for use in the picture was absurd.

It was decided to go with the mechanical shark. A second unit, under Ron and Valerie Taylor, shot film footage of real Great Whites for quick inserts in the picture. The Taylors had done some spectacular underwater photography for Peter Gimbel's documentary, *Blue Water, White Death.*

There was another reason for using a mechanical shark. The fact remained that the Great White in *Jaws*—both novel and film—did not really act like any Great White that had ever existed. Occasionally, a Great White may grow as large as the one in *Jaws* (twenty-five feet long), but there has never been documentation of one with such a long memory and petulant temperment.

Sharks are dispassionate creatures. They don't "go after" particular people or seek revenge on anyone. The shark in *Jaws* is basically a "monster" like the fictional prehistoric "rhedosaurus" that attacks New York in *The Beast From 20,000 Fathoms*, if nowhere near as large.

The mechanical shark was nicknamed "Bruce." There were actually three models, each of which weighed approximately 2000 pounds. The skin was made of polyurethane, and the insides of welded tubular steel, and having flexible joints for movement. One of the models was only used for scenes when the shark had to rush past people and boats in the water. Mounted on a mechanical arm, it rode along a track constructed on the sea bottom. The other two models were operated by the crew using miles of pneumatic hoses which could drive the motors attached to the skeletal armatures.

The models were built by Robert A. Mattey, the retired special effects man who had built the giant squid for the Disney Studio's *Twenty Thousand Leagues Under The Sea.*

Unfortunately, the mechanical sharks did not always prove to be compliant performers. The crew members assigned to handle them had conniption fits as whichever "Bruce" they were working with stubbornly refused to do what he was supposed to. Even worse, they would break down just as a key shooting moment was about to occur.

Mattey's sharks got mixed reviews when the film came out, depending on whether or not a critic could overlook the flaws. Wrote one, "the fact that the villain in *Jaws* is a polyurethane hydraulically-powered mechanical construction doesn't dampen the tension at all." But another said, that "it doesn't help that this facsimile looks like a foam rubber pillow with the zipper open."

To be honest, Mattey's sharks never quite convince you that they're real, but neither are they exactly cheesy. They are effective enough most of the time to create an illusion. Even when the illusion fades, the action helps the viewer "suspend disbelief."

A large part of the picture's success has to go to the actors, who come off as real people instead of "types." Richard Dreyfuss spent so much time in rustic pubs pursuing the local ladies, that Steven was afraid he'd be too tired to act. Luckily, he made fatigue work for him. Roy Scheider was a lot like the character he was playing: not a coward, but very practical.

In the scene when the boat's cabin fills with water as he's trapped inside, Scheider was afraid the crew members might not get him out in time and he'd drown. Although Brody never gets the "bigger boat" he thinks he and the others will need to capture the shark, Scheider himself wasn't about to leave things to chance. He secreted axes on the cabin set so he could get himself out of the rapidly rising water if he had to.

As crusty Quint, the shark hunter, Robert Shaw was playing a more "flamboyant" character than the others in the film, but you couldn't imagine anyone else doing it so well.

Spielberg crafted some exciting scenes for *Jaws* during shooting, but his work was hardly over when filming stopped. In post-production, veteran editor Verna Fields worked her brand of magic. John Williams was brought in to compose what would soon become a famous score with its ominous two-note theme.

During a preview, Spielberg disliked one gruesome moment, when a corpse's head drops into a hole in the hull of a boat and terrifies Dreyfuss swimming below. He was afraid the shock of the moment would be spoiled by showing the actor's reacting to the horror before the audience could see the head. Apparently, simply re-editing would not solve the problem. Steven took his cinematographer and headed for Verna Field's swimming pool.

Ms. Fields was startled, to say the least, when she walked into her backyard and saw that the water in her pool was as cloudy and murky as sea water. Steven had tried to re-create the waters around Martha's Vineyard by pouring in a tub of powdered milk!

When they finished reshooting the underwater scene in the pool with the boat and the body, there were more problems. Ms. Fields reminded Steven that he had broken union rules by failing to use a crew. To his credit, Spielberg fessed up. He was

ordered to make a substantial donation to the union's
retirement fund.

By and large, the critics and public alike were
thrilled with Steven's movie. *Jaws* became a
"monster" hit. On the plus side were such outstanding action sequences as when these two foolhardy
guys use their wives' holdiay roasts to try to snare
the Great White. They're nearly devoured when it
pulls apart the dock they're standing on.The final
scenes where the shark attacking the boat when
Broady, Hooper and Quint try to capture the animal are quite exciting. So are some of the shark-
eats-people scenes.

There are those, however, who felt that while
Jaws was a good, well-made, exciting movie, it was
not outstanding. Part of the reason for this was that
Jaws, despite its well-developed lead characters, had
a lot in common with earlier monster movies. Il-
logic, for instance. The Great White is described
as a "night feeder," but attacks two people during
broad daylight.

Similarly, *Jaws* never works up much compas-
sion for its victims. One could even argue that it
takes a horrible reality—that several people are killed or maimed by sharks each year—and exploits
it for its "entertainment" value. Because Spielberg
at the time was more comfortable with action and

special effects stories than with people stories, he fails to develop what one might call the movie's "theme."

This is that the petrified Chief Brody decides to go with Hooper and Quint to catch the shark because he feels indirectly responsible for the death of a little boy. The boy, who was around the same age as Brody's two sons, was killed by the shark after the mayor refuses Brody's request to close the beaches. The boy's mother learns that Brody knew the danger and slaps him during a confrontation.

While Spielberg makes an attempt to convey Brody's guilt feelings, he seems much more interested in gettng to the next shark attack. As a result, the movie seems rather callous over the boy's horrible death, not to mention everyone else's.

What Speilberg is successful at is in illustrating one of the most fascinating aspects of shark attacks, that they generally occur in only three feet of water. Several scenes demonstrate the horror of being assaulted by a gnashing, carnivorous animal while standing or swimming only a few feet away from land, people, and safety. "Parts of the book terrorized (sic) me," Spielberg has said. "I tried to translate my fear into visual language."

For many viewers, the most chilling part of the movie didn't feature the Great White at all, but was when Quint tells his long, terrible story about the *U.S. S. Indianapolis.* Torpedoed during World War II, the ship sank and 500 men had to wait for rescue in frigid, shark-infested waters. By the time help came, only 316 were left—many of the rest were eaten by sharks. A true story, it was turned into a disturbing movie, *Mission of the Shark,* starring Richard Thomas in 1991.

One month after *Jaws* opened, it had already grossed sixty million dollars. Thus, it was no surprise that the film engendered three sequels (only one of which, *Jaws 3-D,* was even remotely worthwhile), and a whole slew of imitations featuring Makos, Hammerheads, and Tigers. Not to be outdone, other producers came out with films starring bad-tempered octipi, alligators, crocodiles, piranha, mutated barracuda, and every other aquatic creature that could be considered even remotely menacing.

Speilberg had nothing to do with any of these movies. One sea movie was all he needed.

But what about space aliens? That was a different story.

Chapter 4

Alien Encounters

When Steven was a small boy, his father came into his bedroom late one night and woke him up. Without telling him where they were going, his father bundled him into the family car and drove out into the desert. There father and son sat under the sky and watched a meteor shower far overhead. The meteor shower didn't scare Steven; what bothered him was being awakened in the middle of the night and taken off without knowing where he was going.

Since that long-ago night, the sky has never held any terror for Steven Spielberg. That was one reason why the aliens in *Close Encounters of the Third Kind* (1977) were essentially benevolent. Another was that, as he put it, "in all the tens of thousands of UFO reports, none of them are hostile. In my heart, I wanted our encounter to be peaceful." (Actually, in such stories, the aliens hardly act in a "peaceful" manner).

Steven wasn't certain that aliens really existed, but he did believe that many people had had encounters with something outside the ordinary. He had an open mind on the subject.

He had actually written the script for *Close Encounters* (aka *CE3*) before he had gotten the assignment to direct *Jaws*. None of the studios he showed it to thought a movie about friendly aliens would make a dime when most science fiction movies presented outer space visitors with malevolent intentions, such as the would-be conquering Martians of *The War of the Worlds* (1953).

The producers, Julia and Michael Phillips, hired a writer named Paul Schrader (*Taxi Driver*) to punch up Steven's script, but Spielberg disliked what Schrader did to it. "It was not about UFOs at all, it was more about the Church and the State and it was absolutely horrendous." Steven discarded most of Schrader's ideas and went back to his original concept and script.

In the beginning, Spielburg had no intention of letting Richard Dreyfuss, star of *Jaws*, to headline in *Close Encounters*, but he was turned down when he offered the part to such major stars as Jack Nicholson (The Joker in *Batman*), Gene Hackman (Lex Luthor in *Superman*), and Al (*The Godfather*) Pacino. Dreyfuss got the part.

The title of *CE3* comes from a book by Dr. J. Allen Hynek, *The UFO Experience*. In the book Hynek explains that there are three kinds of possible encounters with alien life forms. In the first kind, you simply see an extraterrestrial vehicle. In the second, you find evidence of the spaceship at the site where you saw it. The third kind of contact is actually meeting an alien.

Close Encounters was filmed under a veil of absolute secrecy, in the hopes that no cheap rip-off would be rushed out by an independent producer to compete with it. Every member of the cast and crew had to sign a form that forbade him to give interviews to reporters. No pictures were released that could be used in proposed articles about the movie. No matter how hard the media clamored for information, all they got were vague press releases from the studio.

Things got so bad that when Steven showed up on the set one day without his Security Clearance Badge, the guard on duty didn't recognize him and refused him admittance! Press curiosity got so out-of-hand that a *Time* magazine critic pulled strings to find out where the first sneak preview of the picture was to be held. Learning it was in Texas, he flew down there and told a man waiting in line with a ticket that the preview was a Walt Disney nature short. The man gladly handed over his ticket.

Close Encounters concerns the events surrounding an alien spaceship landing on earth and
an extraterrestrial race making direct contact with
human beings after years of furtive contact. In the
months before the landing, some people who have
seen UFOs are affected more than others. One man
(Richard Dreyfuss) becomes obsessed with a geo-
logical formation that he sees in his mind. He scoops
his mashed potatoes into an odd shape, and tears
up his backyard to build a model of the shape in
his living room. Confused and then angered by his
behavior, his wife takes the kids and leaves him.

Another woman (Melinda Dillon) is also haunt-
ed by the same formation, but she soon forgets that
when her little boy (Cary Cuffey) is kidnapped one
night by the aliens. Independently, she and Dreyfuss
and many others realize that the formation they see
in their minds is really the oddly-shaped Devil's
Tower in Wyoming. Dreyfuss and Dillon join other
UFO observers to find out what's really going on
and get the boy back. They suspect a government
cover-up. At the end of the movie the alien mothership lands near Devil's Tower; when it leaves,
Dreyfuss accompanies the aliens with the
government's blessing.

Diverse special effects techniques were used in

the film, most of them supervised by "FX" wizard, Douglass Trumbull. "The difficulty for me on *Close En-counters* was the sort of bizarre juxtaposition of extremely unusual effects in an extremely ordinary setting," he said when the film was released. $3.5 million was spent on special effects, most of which were created in a special facility set up just for that purpose.

The aliens were played by children who had especially thin arms and legs and who wore masks. Another FX man named Carlo Rimbaldi designed a small moveable puppet for the taller, thinner alien seen in close up. A smaller version of the mothership was built and placed behind the puppet to make it appear life-size.

The mothership was acutaly a "miniature" which was six feet in diameter. Movie miniatures often be a fraction of the size of the real article, but rarely are as small as, say, model cars). The miniature took six months to build, and was full of complicated fibre optics and wiring systems, as well as neon lighting. Other, smaller UFOs seen in the picture were made by taking a basic model and adding different parts to come up with dozens of different types of extraterrestrial vehicles. These miniature alien craft were often photographed against miniature backgrounds, such as a toll booth through which a variety of multi-colored, dazzling UFOs pass. One shot of the Indiana countryside, including trees and buildings, was entirely made up of minatures.

The set for the landing field near Devil's Tower where the mothership comes down was so big that no Hollywood soundstage—where large sets are usually erected—could possibly hold it. It could not be done in miniature, as dozens of extras had to mill around on the set. The producer found a huge, abandoned airplane hangar located in Mobile, Alabama; even this wasn't big enough. They had to add a 150-foot tent to one end of the hangar so that everything could fit within: buildings, planes, people, the rocks surrounding everything, and of course the not-so-small miniatures of the various spaceships.

Another special effects technique that was heavily employed in *CE3* was matte painting. To save money and not have to build extensive sets, filmmakers often call in special artists who can paint realistic scenery and structures which are placed iside—or "matted" into—the "live-action" (or real) visual image. Thus, the crew can build, say, the first story of a tall edifice, and the rest of the stories can simply be painted and blended into the shot.

The Devil's Tower hangar/landing field set was

surrounded by matte art of trees and hills in some long shots for added veracity. Matte paintings were also used in certain night shots to supply backgrounds to the farmhouse from which the little boy is kidnapped. Some shots of the night sky and stars were also matte paintings to approximate the desired effect.

When the film was released, it got mostly respectful reviews—apart from a few dissensions—and went on to make over a quarter of a million dollars in profits. Two years later, Spielberg wanted to tinker a little bit more with the movie, and made several changes to the picture. He was given a million to film new scenes with Richard Dreyfuss. These scenes now showed him entering the well-lit Cathedral-like interior of the mothership. An earlier new scene showed him freaking out in front of his wife and child. Another added sequence showed the aliens skyjacking a ship and its entire crew and depositing same in the Mongolian desert. Several cuts were made to the film as well, i.e., the scenes when Dreyfuss obsessively tears up his backyard.

Some critics felt that Spielberg had no right to make changes in a film that had already been released and seen by millions of people. One reviewer noted: "If an artist can revise a film every few years, we'll never get a finished piece, merely a slew of perpetual works in progress that will be impossible to judge in context."

CE3 is a good, entertaining movie but not a masterpiece. On the plus side, the movie has an eerieness and a sense of wonder that the more recent *Independence Day* lacks, and it deals with government cover-ups about aliens years before TV's *X Files* did the same. The effects and cinematography are excellent, and *Close Encounters* is best seen on a large screen in a movie theater. Some of the scenes are particularly exciting: Dreyfuss and Dillon climbing up Devil's Tower dodging helicopters, and the approach of the mothership toward the landing site as it positively dwarfs the whole mountain. John Willliams' musical score adds a certain magical lustre to the finale.

On the debit side, sometimes it seems as if *CE3* is about nothing but effects. The characters are rather one-dimensional, there are tedious sections in the middle of the film (some of which were cut for the "special edition"), and the movie seems to end too suddenly. We never learn where the aliens are from or exactly what they're after.

Speaking of those aliens, Spielberg considers them "benign" and friendly, but some of their actions are anything but. What purpose is served in the kidnapping the little boy and utterly terrorizing the boy's mother when they come for him in the night? Why did they spirit away several planes reported missing in 1945, and only return their pilots to earth over thirty years later (no older than they were when they left.)?

On this point, Spielberg has said: "I would like to see what happens when the twenty-two-year-old pilot knocks on the door, and his children are grown and they have kids and their kids have kids." But what if these pilots discover that everyone they've ever cared about has died in their absence? What's "benign" about doing that to someone? Of course, in the "special edition," the aliens also steal a ship out of the ocean and drop it in the desert, hardly a friendly gesture, even if no one is killed. Spielberg put these scenes in because they were intriguing, but he didn't realize that they would also make his aliens–and his movie—seem pretty senseless. These mysterious doings keep the viewer watching but, as one critic put it, "if only there were a powerful story to thread it all together!"

Many people thought it stretched belief that Dreyfuss would go off in the mothership with the aliens at the end of the film. Sure, he might be embarking on a great—or terrible—adventure, but what about his wife and children? Even if his relationship with his wife has been irreparably damaged, surely he doesn't want to let as long as thirty years go by before he sees his kids again? Spielberg made the film before having children of his own, and says that he would have ended the film differently had he made it today."(Dreyfuss) is totally irresponsible to his family to pursue his obsession," he says

Spielberg's next project—and also his first critical and (comparatively) financial failure—was a picture entitled *1941*. This was a wartime comedy about an hysterical reaction in California after the bombing of Pearl Harbor. Certain residents of Los Angeles are convinced the Japanese's next bombing site will be their very own city and respond to the imagined threat in varying ways. Many people felt that the basic premise of the film was tasteless.

Spielberg owed Universal Studios one more picture after *Jaws*, and he enjoined them to let him film the script. Columbia Studios, under whose auspices *CE3* was filmed, decided to co-finance the expensive picture. The budget kept getting higher and higher—20, 30, 40 million—as tongues began wagging that Spielberg had bitten off more than he could chew. As filming proceeded, he began to agree with them. Too late he realized that *1941* wasn't really his kind of picture, even though it had looked good on paper. He would eventually say, "I'll spend the rest of my life disowning this movie." This time he tinkered with the film—especially the first forty-five minutes—before its release, but to no avail. (Most of the cut scenes were put back in for a three-hour television showing).

The trouble with *1941* is that it's too long, busy and overblown. Some very effective comedic sequences are buried amid an awful lot of noisy scenes of slapstick and destruction. John Williams' score is too heavy and ponderous. However, there are moments when Steven's flair for staging big, brassy crowd and action scenes are much in evidence. As usual in a Spielberg film, the special effects are the highlight, such as when a ferris wheel rolls down a dock and splashes into the ocean. The talented cast does its best to be amusing, but the film is only a cut above mediocre.

Still, *1941* was not the mega-bomb everyone predicted. It didn't make anywhere near the money of *Jaws* or *CE3*, but it did break even—with a few million to spare.

Chapter 5

The Adventures of Indiana

George (*Star Wars*) Lucas and Steven Spielberg had known each other for years, but had never worked together. Both had been fans of cliffhanger serials when they were boys. In these serials, generally shown on Saturday afternoons in movie theaters, heroes like *Captain Marvel* or *The Lone Ranger* would battle nefarious villains in twelve to fifteen chapters shown over as many weeks. Lucas and Spielberg hoped to put all of the thrills of an entire fifteen week serial into one motion picture.

The basic plot of the film that resulted—*Raiders of the Lost Ark* (1981)—was lifted from a 1943 Republic serial entitled, *The Secret Service in Darkest Africa*. In both the old serial and the new movie there was an American hero and Nazi villains who were after ancient artifacts. In *Raiders*, the artifact was the Lost Ark of the Covenant containing the tablets of the Ten Commandments. Lucas would be would be executive producer, while Steven did the directorial honors.

Despite their friendship, Lucas had noted how the production—and costs—of *1941* had become so overblown. He told Steven he would have to watch the spending and suggested storyboards for the film (each shot would be planned in advance in a kind of comic strip). This technique worked so well for Spielberg that he brought the film in early and at only half the prescribed budget.

The hero of the film was supposed to have been a kind of James Bond-type ladykiller, but instead became a bespectacled archaeology professor who somehow manages to turn into a dashing hero who doesn't need his glasses. Harrison Ford was cast in the role.

In some ways, Indiana Jones was similar to the sometimes ruthless, expedient anti-heroes of those old serials. More than one critic noted that what he does is "steal cultural artifacts." Confronted with a swordsman who plans to slice and dice him, Indiana pulls his gun and shoots him dead without a second thought. (The swordsman would have had no compunction about killing Indiana). In contrast, the movie's heroine (Karen Allen) manages to get away from an assailant with a knife and bops him on the head with a pan—disarming him without killing him.

The scene with the swordsman came about because on the day of shooting Harrison Ford was suffering from "Montezuma's revenge," a stomach problem that affects tourists in Tunisia (where they were filming) and elsewhere. Ford was in no shape to spend a lot of time away from his hotel room. To accommodate him, Spielberg had him simply shoot his opponent instead of choreographing and filming the more complicated battle that had been planned.

Spielberg wanted to cast his girlfriend, actress Amy Irving, in the role of Marian Ravenwood, who helps Indiana against the Nazis, but they had one of several break-ups before filming began. Karen Allen got the part but didn't care for how her role was written. Because of this, she and Spielberg did not get along very well, and she and her character were written out of the sequel.

Raiders of the Lost Ark is a very entertaining movie, but somehow not the real classic it could have been. Perhaps because Indiana is such a one-dimensional character. One thing that can't be argued with is that Spielberg crafted some truly wonderful action sequences for the film. The prologue alone is worth the price of admission.

In the opening sequence, Indiana and a com-

panion must pass through several traps to reach a
hidden chamber where Indiana finds the artifact he
is seeking. Trapdoors over bottomless pits open in
the stone floor of the tunnel; spears with impaled
skeletons attached suddenly swoosh out of the walls.
The *piece de resistance* is a gigantic round rock that
bursts out of a wall and rolls relentlessly after a
fleeing Indiana, who narrowly misses being crush-
ed beneath its weight.

The rock was built full-size and was twelve feet
high. An actual rock that size would weigh several
tons, but the replica wasn't exactly as light as a
feather. Filled with wood and plaster and with a
fiberglass covering, it was over 300 pounds. Refus-
ing to use a stunt double, Ford was nearly flat-
tened by the rock during filming.

Another great sequence features a tomb which
is full of skeletons and snakes, one of which slithers
out of the mouth of a skull as Marian screams. Indiana has an exciting battle with a bald giant peri-
lously close to an airplane's propeller as the Nazis
approach and a stream of gasoline underneath the
plane threatens to ignite any second. The bit with
Indiana pulling himself along the undercarriage of
a speeding truck is a memorable (if hard-to-believe)
sequence. And the special effects of the finale—in
which the "light" from the ark disintegrates the

villains—are impressive.

The film has plenty of humor as well. Such as when an ugly little man approaches the imprisoned Marian threateningly, all the while fiddling with a sinister metal device that turns out not to be an instrument of torture but a collapsible coat hanger. In another scene, Marian gives Indiana a passionate kiss, only to have him fall asleep on her. Indiana is no James Bond lover boy, that's for sure.

Raiders of the Lost Ark was a spectacular success, grossing over $360 million! Steven had promised George Lucas that if the film did well, he would make a couple of more sequels. Although he had only agreed to this with a handshake, he kept his word (why should he argue with success?). The sequel was entitled *Indiana Jones and the Temple of Doom* (1984).

In *Temple of Doom*, beginning in Shanghai in 1935, Indiana is hooked up with a new lady named Willie (Kate Capshaw), and a boy named Short Round (Ke Huy Quan). This intrepid trio wind up in India, where they put the kibosh on a horrible cult that enslaves children and forces them to work in undergound mines.

Temple of Doom is probably the best of the trilogy of Indiana Jones films, but when it was released Spielberg was amazed to learn that many people found it controversial. The reason for this was a sequence late in the film when the heart of a human sacrifice is torn out by the leader of the cult.

The outrage over the sequence was inexplicable to many people. There were plenty of gruesome scenes in *Raiders*—the melting faces of the Nazis, for instance—and the offensive sequence in *Temple of Doom* is presented in such an "unreal" way that it doesn't seem truly graphic. The priest's hand—and the heart in its grip—sort of passes through the victim's chest as if he were immaterial, making the whole business unpleasant, perhaps, but hardly repulsive.

Much more disturbing to many viewers was the sequence where Indiana and Willie are trapped in a hidden chamber which is full of exotic insects. Spielberg sent out a call for 20,000 of the ugliest, biggest, and most disgusting bugs that exist anywhere in the world. When she saw them, Kate Capshaw hated the idea (as most people would) of letting the little darlings crawl all over her. She said she would do the scene if Steven himself stood beside her in the insect-filled enclosure out of camera range. He agreed to do so, and it was one of the least pleasant situations he had ever found himself in.

Again Amy Irving had been up for the role of

Indiana's leading lady, but another falling out with Steven led to his casting Capshaw. For a while Spielberg was romantically torn between the two actresses, but married Irving in 1985. The two had a son named Max. The marriage lasted only four years for many reasons, among them the months of separation while each worked on different film projects. After divorcing Irving, Spielberg married Kate Capshaw, in 1991.

There were also complaints that Capshaw's character in *Temple of Doom* is a far cry from the more heroic or "liberated" heroine of Marian Ravenwood in the first film. Willie seems to spend most of her time screaming. But Willie was conceived as an ordinary person, a kind of Everywoman, who reacts to these astonishing events (insects and whatnot) as most of us, male or female, would: with a screech of horror. The fact that Willie is able to overcome her terror and help Indie destroy the cult makes her that much more admirable than if she had been a brave Wonder Woman from the start.

For the stunts in *Temple of Doom*, Spielberg borrowed from old serials such as *Tiger Woman* (1944) and *King of the Mounties* (1942). Once, Indiana escapes from pursuers by cutting the ropes that support the suspension bridge on which he and his opponents are standing. The pursuers plummet into the waters of the gorge as Indiana holds onto the ends of the ropes and swings safely to the other side. It must be said that while the basic situation is the same as in the old movies, this sequence in *Temple* is far more effective than those similar scenes in the cliffhangers of yesteryear. *Temple* proceeds at a breathless pace with one thrilling peril after another being thrown at the heroes and at the audience.

Critics who felt some scenes in *Raiders* that stretched belief couldn't help but notice that occasionally *Temple* veered into out-and-out fantasy. *Raiders* fans wondered how Indie could survive on top—and outside—of a submarine for such a long voyage, but at least the sub is never shown submerging. In *Temple*, however, a bit when Indie and company jump out of a plane and survive is as believable as a roadrunner cartoon. But the film is so much fun that nobody really cared.

Responding to his critics, Spielberg practically disowned the film years later. He said it was too dark and sinister for his taste. "There's not an ounce of my own personal feeling in *Doom*," he said.

Indiana Jones to date has had one more screen appearance in *Indiana Jones and the Last Crusade* (1989), the most disappointing of the series, although it got better reviews than *Temple of Doom*.

One problem is that *Last Crusade* seems like a remake of *Raiders of the Lost Ark*, with the hero again combating Nazis and searching for a mystical treasure. The film is perfectly acceptable, Spielberg's direction workmanlike, but the film has only one standout sequence. This occurs when Indiana has a battle on a runaway tank as it heads toward the edge of a cliff. The first James Bond, Sean Connery, was brought in to play Indiana's father.

The picture was filmed in the south of Spain in Almeria, with additional shooting at the Elstree Studios in London and some more location work in Colorado. Some of the FX techniques employed included animatronics (a mechanical rhinoceros which bedevils Indie) and a stop-motion (a frame-by-frame animated puppet of a lion). The sets in London included a huge temple built for the climax. It was over 80 feet tall and covered with imitation gold. A miniatured temple was blown up for the finale.

Spielberg plans to direct a fourth Indiana Jones film (in which star Harrison Ford intends to participate), but it has yet to materialize. In 1991 George Lucas became executive producer of the *Young Indiana Jones Chronicles,* an ABC television series wich lasted a couple of years. The series consisted of twenty or so hour-long episodes and several two-hour "movies." Sean Patrick Flannery got the part of young Indiana when the late River Phoenix, who played the role in *Last Crusade*, decided to pass.

Lucas was asked if Spielberg would have anything to do with the TV show. "He is consulted," said Lucas. "He's obviously an interested party because he was so involved in the features. He's aware of what's going on and I've talked to him about doing an episode." However, Spielberg never directed any episodes of the show.

Chapter 6

Phoning Home

While making *Raiders of the Lost Ark* and still stinging from the poor returns for *1941*, Spielberg was planning another film. The profits from *Close Encounters of the Third Kind* had been so huge that he figured a sequel would certainly put him back on top (if *Raiders* didn't work out). If *Close Encounters* friendly extraterrestrials, the sequel would feature aliens who were decidedly malevolent.

By this time Steven had been alerted to the fact that many so-called "encounters" between humans and space aliens were of a definitely nightmarish quality. In particular there was the old story of a backwoods Kentucky family in the 1950s. They had allegedly been terrorized by a group of aliens who invaded their home and nearly carried the whole family off with them. This gave Steven the basic scenario: a family fighting off extraterrestrial barbarians.

The studio gave the project the green light.

Spielberg only intended to produce the movie; a production designer named Ron Bobb was to direct. John Sayles, author of many genre films while directing more "serious" features of his own, was drafted to write a script. Speieberg also contacted make-up artist Rick Baker (*An American Werewolf in London*) to bring the film's aliens to life.

There were eleven aliens with different personalities and features. One as a "badass" called Scar. An alien who looked deceptively benign was named Squirt. The pivotal creature was a genuinely sympathetic alien called "Buddy." It was this character who eventually turned into the star of *E.T.*

Spielberg's new project was retitled *Night Skies* while filming proceeded on *Raiders of the Lost Ark*. Eventually, Steven got different ideas about what the picture should actually be about. "I was sitting there in the middle of Tunisia, scratching my head and saying, 'I've got to get back to the tranquility, or at least the spirituality, of *CE3*...' My reaction was to immediately think of a very touching and tender relationship developing between an extraterrestrial and an eleven-year-old child who takes him in."

Harrison Ford's girlfriend, Melissa Mathison, had come to visit Ford in Tunisia, and Steven told her his idea. She was so enthusiastic, or at least pretended to be, that Spielberg hired her to do the new screenplay on the spot. (In Hollywood, connections never hurt). As this had become a more personal film, Spielberg decided to direct it himself. Cobb, Sayles, and Baker were informed there would be no more *Night Skies* and that was that.

This new film was first called, *A Boy's Life*. Spielberg recalled that when he was sixteen, "my imagination took me to places that felt good...I needed a special friend." The premise was culled from Spielberg's own loneliness he felt on the set of *Raiders* in Tunisia. (He may have been surrounded by the people in both instances, but a person can still feel loneliness even in a crowd). Basing the character upon himself, he created a boy who needs a friend and finds one in a lonely lost alien from space.

But one person thought the idea for *E.T.* came from somewhere other than Spielberg's head. Playwright Lisa Marie Litchfield claimed that the storyline for *E.T.* was stolen from her one-act musical play, *Lokey from Maldemar*. She sued for $750 million in U.S. District Court. The play ran in Los Angeles for a brief time and was submitted to Universal Pictures (which released *E.T.*) for review. There were several plot similarities between the two works. An out-of-court settlement was reached.

In *E.T.*, Elliott (Henry Thomas) encounters a friendly alien who was left behind when his companions took off in their spaceship. Government agents are looking for the alien—dubbed *E.T.* for "extraterrestrial"—who wonders if he can use an earth telephone to "phone home" to his friends. Despite his special powers, such as levitation, telepathy, and healing powers, *E.T.* appears to die. But he revives in time to make it to the returning spaceship and rejoin the other aliens. Elliott knows he has made a lasting friend from the other end of the universe.

Spielberg had difficulty finding a boy to play Elliott, and the actor he chose, nine-year-old Henry Thomas, gave a terrible first reading. Once he got over his nervousness, however, Thomas impressed Spielberg so much that he hired him on the spot. Dee Wallace (Stone) played Elliott's mother; she quarreled with Spielberg when he told her that *E.T.* was the star of the film and not her. To retaliate, she orchestrated a campaign to get an Oscar nomination, although she had very little to do with the film.

Spielberg has often been accused of being willing destroy the careers of actors who cross him. Those who believe this cite the fact that the careers of Karen Allen, Amy Irving, and Dee Wallace didn't amount to much after their appearances in highly-touted Spielberg movies. But the acting business is a merciless one and a particular actor's fortunes rise and fall for a variety of reasons. Spielberg is still happily married to Kate Capshaw, and her career has hardly set the world on fire.

In any case, the true star of *E.T.* was the alien. Much of the $10.5 million budget (which was actually fairly low) was spent on bringing the extraterrestrial to life. This was done with a variety of techniques. Carlo Rambaldi, who created the aliens for *Close Encounters*, was asked to work his magic with *E.T.* when things didn't work out with Rick Baker. Now that *Night Skies* had become *A Boy's Life*, the old contract was no longer valid, and disputes between Baker and Spielberg disintegrated into screaming matches and the two would not work together on the film.

Rambaldi built three models of E.T. in his "electronic manual proportional system." The first model was electronic and was capable of eighty-five individual movements. A much lighter electro-mechanical model could simulate sixty life-like movements. A third model was radio-controlled and was only used in scenes with the other aliens. Two models were made to move via cables that led off forty-five feet out of camera range. Anywhere from two to twelve assistants operated the controls. Levers would control the hydraulic system that made the models move. The neck stretched, the eyes bulged, the tongue stuck out, as if E.T. were really alive.

Make-up artist Craig Reardon painted the models' rubber skin to achieve the proper out-of-this-world look, rather leathery and patchy. Sculptor Robert Short created E.T.'s chest, where the heart lights up and could be seen through his skin. "We built soft organs to act like balloons," said Short. "We pumped air in and out of them to make them beat, and put them all on a plexiglass sheet. We put a quartz-halogen light behind that to get the intensity we needed, and then ran an air conditioning unit through the whole thing."

A midget named Pat Bilon also played E.T. in certain sequences, such as when the alien is running or walking, or, as Bilon put it, "chasing Drew Barrymore. In the bicycle basket, being chased by the FBI agents, it was me." Bilon wore another four-piece Rambaldi suit which contained a battery pack, mechanized parts, and special controls. Bilon could manipulate some of the parts of the suit himself, while others, such as the fingers, were moved by remote control. The suit was very heavy for Bilon and once caught on fire while he was still wearing it. But fortunately, Bilon noticed the problem before he was injured.

"Pat Bilon is the most cooperative and gentlest person I have ever met," Spielberg said when filming was over. For his part, Bilon said, "I wanted to help give E.T. a person-ality. Something people could identify with."

Finally, a stunt woman named Tamara de Treaux played E.T. in one brief scene, when E.T. climbs up the runway on the spaceship. Rambaldi was furious when she told reporters she alone had brought E.T. to life, a patently false claim considering all the FX work that went into figuratively animating the little creature.

Industrial Light and Magic (I.L.M.) did the other special effects, including the optical work. (Optical effects imply a manipulation of film itself, as opposed to mechanical effects, which are shot live. E.T.'s spaceship is a two-foot wide model which lands in a miniature-set forest. Ralph McQuarrie's design for the ship, which was controlled by a computer, incorporated a lot of detail work. An additional model, three feet wide with much less detail, was built for long shots.

The movie's most magical scenes are an optical effect using a number of techniques. These, of course, are when E.T. uses his powers to make bicycles and riders fly through the air and across the moon. With the exception of some close-ups, the actors were replaced with miniature models of both themselves and the bikes they're riding. These were animated with a special process called "go-motion," a variation of stop-motion.

In the latter, a model is animated frame-by-frame but remains perfectly still during each shot (it appears to move when the shots are run together). In go-motion, the model is moved a bit during each shot so that a blurring occurs (which happens during normal filming), making the model look more realistic These models or puppets were then photographed in front of a blue screen. Later on, the background—the moon, for instance—would be added to achieve the final effect.

When *E.T.* was released, the critical reaction was almost universally positive. Critics fell all over themselves singing the movie's praises. The formidable *Cinefantastique* magazine ran a review that read like a press release from Universal's publicty office. *Life* magazine proclaimed Spielberg a genius on the level of Mozart! One reviewer swore that E.T. was meant to be Jesus Christ and that the whole movie was a re-telling of certain chapters in the Bible.

To say that much of the praise was comically overdone would be an understatement, even if the film was indeed quite charming on first viewing. It was also heavily hyped by the studio.

There were some naysayers, however, *Cinefantastique*'s critic Tim Lucas wrote: "Deep down, where its going to count, when Time wears away its surface sweetness, *E.T.* is a spoiled brat's movie; one that America's eye has been too occluded with Kleenex to view objectively."

David Bathrolomew wrote: "At the point when the film could show some of the real sadness that exists and must be faced in the world, it opts out for cheap sentiment. And this can do a lot of damage to ethical attitudes. When a master filmmaker like Spielberg constructs such a powerful statement that touches some of our basic concerns, and then pulls back into escapist pablum, it tends to reinforce the desire for easy answers to complex problems."

George Lucas reportedly loved the bit when *E.T.* begins to follow a child wearing a Yoda (*The Empire Strikes Back*) mask, but was less thrilled when his friend's movie surpassed *Star Wars* to become the top-grossing film of all time (up to 1982). A good sport, Lucas publicly chided the Academy for failing to give Steven an academy award for *E.T.* ,but Spielberg himself said, "*E.T.* is my favorite movie, but it's not my best-directed film." (He thought *CE3* was his best directorial performance)

E.T. made millions of extra dollars through merchandising, selling diverse items related to the movie. Everyone thought that *Swamp Thing*, also released that year, would bring in the biggest merchandising bucks, but the picture was easily swamped by *E.T.*

A bigger loser was Mars, the company that manufactures M&Ms. When the studio asked permission for Elliott to use M&Ms in the scene when he uses candy to attract the alien out of hiding, Mars said no. Instead, Elliott uses Reese's Pieces, manufactured by Hershey. The makers of M&Ms lost a billion dollars in free advertising, and sales for Reese's Pieces, went up by 65%. Sales for E.T. dolls, masks, and stuffed toys were also spectacular.

Regardless of how much money *E.T.* made, the picture is hardly without its flaws. For one thing, it lacks a true sense of wonder. E.T. is a creature from another planet, yet he could have been just a weird pet from another continent the way the movie treats him. Elliott and the rest of his family are one-dimensiional characters. The children act like real kids all right, but they have no identities. If Spielberg's inspiration was a lonely child, that does not come across in his movie. Elliott isn't lonely, unhappy, full of fantasy, or even an only child. He's merely a cypher.

Spielberg manages to portray the world from the viewpoint of a tiny, terrified alien with great clarity. Otherwise, his direction seems a trifle slow-paced and ordinary. John Williams' score is effective, but there are times when the composer seems to think he's scoring grand opera instead of a simple fantasy film. Still, there are some amusing and effective sequences, and it's easy to see why the picture has become a favorite of so many children of all ages.

"If I could leave only one film for my kids," says Spielberg, "it would be E.T."

A young Steven directs formidable Joan Crawford on the set of "Night Gallery."

Steven clowns around in one of the hydraulic sharks on the "Jaws" set. Not all moments on the set were this playful.

Spielberg works with close friend Whoopi Goldberg to convey the right mood for her character in "The Color Purple."

Steven poses with the "star" of "E. T."

The big boulder in "Raiders of the Lost Ark" nearly crushes Indiana Jones—and actor Harrison Ford.

Mrs. Freeling (JoBeth Williams) finds corpes in her swimming pool in "Poltergeist."

The evil Gremlins sing Christmas Carols while wreaking havoc in "Gremlins."

The mothership prepares to land at The Devils Tower in "Close Encounters of the Third Kind."

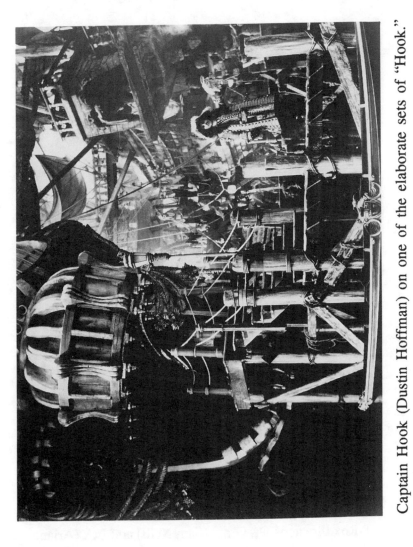

Captain Hook (Dustin Hoffman) on one of the elaborate sets of "Hook."

A T-Rex threatens Dr. Grant (Sam Neill) and Lex (Ariana Richards) in "Jurassic Park."

Spielberg directs Liam Neeson on location in Poland for "Schindler's List."

Steven after receiving an Oscar for "Schindler's List," the first of his more serious films.

Chapter 7

Rabbits, Spiders and Gremlins

Like many directors, Steven Spielberg wanted to have as much control over his pictures as possible. There were also many projects he wanted to bring to fruition but which he didn't have the time to direct personally. Therefore he decided that he would not only produce many of his own movies, but other films which would be directed by different people. Spielberg also formed his own production company called Amblin (for his early film, *Amblin'*), while other movies were done under the auspices of Steven Spielberg Productions.

Spielberg has been executive producer of dozens of movies, but his level of participation is different for each film. Some films are simply put out by his production company and other Amblin employees supervise day-to-day activities. Sometimes Spielberg acts as the "line" producer and oversees every possible aspect of a production, being on the set at all times and even having final say over how the footage will be edited. In cases like this, some people believe Spielberg actually functions as the film's true director regardless of who's name is on the credits.

As director, Spielberg decides what will be shot and how. The director, often consulting with the cinematographer and FX people, decides how to cover the action in each sequence, and which angles will be used. Some directors have a more personal stamp than others, even overseeing the editing of their film. Others are mere employees and are not consulted in such matters as casting or have any say in the final cut of the picture.

As producer, Spielberg makes sure all the other business is taken care of so that the director can do his or her job. Casting, hiring, firing, choosing and securing locations and permission to use them, anything and everything, even to hiring the caterer. The director handles the artistic end while the producer handles the day-to-day business that must be seen to before filming can begin.

Spielberg's initial work as executive producer was for a 1978 comedy entitled, *I Wanna Hold Your Hand*. In this highly entertaining picture, several teens try to get in to see their idols, The Beatles, when the Liverpool foursome are appearing on the *Ed Sullivan Show* in New York. Director Robert

Zemeckis kept things moving at a brisk pace and developed an excellent relationship with Spielberg; the two would collaborate on many films.*Used Cars* (1980), another comedy, was one of them.

Of all the films he has produced, Speilberg was probably most involved behind-the-scenes in *Poltergeist* (1982). In this film, a family moves into a new housing development, unaware that it was over a cemetery.The tombstones were removed, but not the bodies. At first, the ghostly forces at work are more mischievious than malevolent, but things turn ugly when the little girl is sucked into a maelstrom in her bedroom closet. Psychic investigators are called in to get the girl back from whatever netherworld she was taken to as well as to de-haunt the house. The child is returned, but all hell breaks loose before the picture is over.

Spielberg fashioned his story (he also co-wrote the screenplay) from memories of his own childhood fears. In his bedroom there had been a crack in the wall; lying in the darkness, he used to imagine all manner of grotesque and loathesome creatures pouring out of it while he slept. They would drag him back to their domain. Another fear he had was of a clown doll, and often had nightmares that the tree outside his bedroom window would come to "life" to drag him out of the window with one of its branches. All of these things occur in *Poltergeist*.

Again, there were those who felt the film did not come entirely from Spielberg's genius. Actor Paul Clemens and his co-writer Bennett Michael Yellin claimed they had submitted a script to Spielberg's production office which had virtually the same plot, premise, and story elements—a missing daughter, murderous tree, and so on—as the screenplay for *Poltergeist*. When the writer/director Frank DeFelitta saw Spielberg's script, he noticed similarities between one scene and a sequence in his own movie, *The Entity*. Spielberg immediately changed the script when he heard about it.

The special effects crew was really kept busy for *Poltergeist*. A special $40,000 gimbal was built that could rotate an entire room 360 degrees. The cameraman and his camera were fastened down and the actors and student people were hung on wires. This revolving room was used to make it look as if people were levitating or crawling up walls and across ceilings. It was also used in the scene when everything in the little girl's bedroom is sucked into her closet, including the girl and her mother (JoBeth Williams).

The closet door was actually a "miniature" half the size of a real door. "Veins" of a gelatinous material were placed on either side of the doorway. According to producer Frank Marshall, a lot of techniques were used in this sequence. "There were lighting effects, strobes, Las Vegas spots, fishtanks of water to give a different type of diffusion to the beams coming out, four large wind machines, minutiae and smoke. We had to coordinate all that just for a simple effect."

Behind the door was an "esophagus" or throat—a half-scale miniature—in which hoses pumped air into flesh-like material to make it look as if the mouth were breathing. The esophagus was made of acrylic plastic, silicon rubber and polyurethane foam, as well as bubble packaging material, and was illuminated by lights with colored gels. This is one effect in the film that looks a little cheesy. The half-size door was used in a much better scene when a hideous "horror head"—which was only about two feet long—rushes out of the closet at the frightened father (Craig Nelson). Because the head and doorway were placed closer to the camera, the head apppeared to be as big or bigger than the actor.

The tree that pulls the young boy out of the window came in several varieties. A fiberglass model was used for scenes when the tree didn't move. Another one with a metal arm had pneumatic cylinders that could move its limbs as if they were

fingers. The branches were real, covered with a special foam latex skin for added eeriness. The tree's
"mouth" was built so that it could also move, and
a mixture of cornstarch and honey was pumped out
it like floral saliva. One set of branch arms was used
to pick the boy up off his bed, another to pull him
out of the window (he was in a flying harness), and
a third to stuff him into the tree's "mouth."

The scene when the mother turns her back for
a second and looks around to see that all the kitchen chairs have been piled atop one another was
accomplished more easily. A pyramid of chairs had
been bolted together earlier. When the camera panned in the other direction, the pyramid was thrust
into place while the rest of the crew grabbed the
loose chairs and pulled them out of camera range.
To make a kitchen chair slide across the floor as
if it were being pulled by a ghost, the crew built
a raised set with a track underneath the floor that
the chair could be pulled along.

Another set was built upon springs, so that the
family's bedroom could really rock when the
phantoms cause an earthquake. Motors in the walls
made them vibrate, and jets of air hidden on shelves
and bookcases knocked items onto the floor. The
items that fly around the children's bedroom were
filmed with a motion-control camera and then

superimposed over a shot of the bedroom.

Craig Reardon and James Burns made the corpses that pop out of the ground at the end of the film by putting prosthetics and make-up on real human skeletons. A huge trench was dug on location in Simi Valley, inside which coffins, corpses, and technical equipment were buried. At the proper moment, special air machines thrust the coffins right out of the ground for a memorable effect. A pool and a doorway were built at MGM studios for the scenes when a coffin comes through a door and corpses poke up out of the swimming pool.

When the family's home collapses at the finale, Spielberg used a 3x4x5 foot miniature. This doll-size house was made of plastic, foam board and balsa wood, and was filled with tiny pieces of furniture. Cables broke the house apart as it was photographed on its back in a funnel. High-speed cameras slowed down the action for more impact and the footage was eventually matted (placed within) a shot of a vacant lot.

The gruesome (dream) sequence of the parapsychologist's face falling apart as he looks in the mirror was one with a mask made of gelatin-flesh, or "necroderm." Blood was pumped through tubes as the face mask disintegrated. The "crawling steak" was made of foamed plastic and its "guts" were melted vinyl spit out of a grease gun. An artist named Annette Little made the evil clown doll out of clay.

Poltergeist was directed by Tobe Hooper, but because Spielberg had so much control it was rumored that the latter was the true director. This was unfair to Hooper, a very talented filmmaker who had made the *Texas Chainsaw Massacre* before *Poltergeist* and later the science-fiction thriller *Lifeforce*. Despite its gruesome nature, *Chainsaw* had a reputation for graphic violence it did not deserve (everything was actually left to the imagination). And *Lifeforce* was savaged by critics even though it was a highly entertaining and well-made motion picture.

Left to his own devices, there is no doubt that Hooper could have turned out an even better version of *Poltergeist*. *Chainsaw* and *Lifeforce* have atmosphere, and *Poltergeist* has very little. The movie is never believable, and at times seems like a rehash of *The Amityville Horror*. Even the special effects work is uneven. On the plus side, there are a lot of effective, shocking sequences, and the climax with the corpses and imploding house is quite dramatic. But Spielberg had nothing to do with the sequels.

Gremlins (1984) and *Gremlins 2: The New Batch*

(1990) were both brought out by Spielberg's Amblin Productions and directed by Joe Dante. These are comedy-thrillers featuring cuddly, furry creatures, called Mogwai. Under certain conditions, the Mogwai turn into ugly, sinister monsters that revel in malevolence.

The original *Gremlins* was to have been a straight horror film. Parts of the original script remain, such as when the heroine (Phoebe Cates) tells the hero (Zach Galligan) the grotesque story of her father's death. Playing Santa Claus, he broke his neck climbing down the chimney and wasn't discovered until days later when they were alerted by the odor of his decaying body. A high school professor is apparently eaten by the creatures, and an old lady is propelled out of her home by a motorized chair that's doctored by the evil Mogwai. This last scene was played for laughs once it was decided to make *Gremlins* more of a spoof than a terror flick.

Even this charming fantasy film came in for its share of controversy. Some critics objected to the violence, such as when a mother cooks some of the evil Mogwai in her microwave. Surely this is too graphic for little children, they wondered. Actually, most of the kids thought the sequence was hilarious. It's not as if the mother were microwaving kittens, after all. Other critics saw the picture as a commentary on small-town white suburbia being overrun by inner city ghetto youths, which (they theorized) the evil Mogwai were meant to represent. It is unlikely that Spielberg had this in mind while making the picture.

The sequel is even more of a parody, as the Mogwai try to take over an entire office building in Manhattan. In some sequences the actors had to react to creatures that wouldn't be added to the shot until many months later. In other scenes, the Mogwai were always present. Actor Christopher Lee recalled "a scene in the lab at the picture, where they take control. So you've got twenty or thirty Gremlins swarming all over me, each one operated off-camera by three or four people. It was very demanding technically." The Mogwai models were mechanized and controlled by operators outside camera range. "I've never enjoyed making a film more," said Lee.

Spielberg had a minor cameo in *Gremlins*, as he had in *The Blues Brothers*. The only time he's ever appeared on camera for more than a few seconds is in *Listen Up: The Lives of Quincy Jones* (1990), in which he is interviewed.

In 1985, Spielberg worked with director and old friend Robert Zemeckis on the first *Back to the Future* Film. There wasn't a studio that wanted to make the film until Steven got involved. Eric Stolz had originally been cast in the lead, but Spielberg replaced him with Michael J. Fox when he felt Stolz was playing the comedy part too intensely. The film was so popular that two sequels were made.

The theme of the *Future* movies is time travel. In the first film, Fox goes back in time to meet his parents when they were teenagers. His own mother falls in love with him, and Fox is afraid she won't go on the first date with his father that will lead to their marriage. In that case, he won't even be born! It all works out in the end, with the help of the mad scientist, Doc (Christopher Lloyd), who invented the time-spanning automobile in which they travel.

In *Back to the Future 2* (1989), Lloyd and Fox travel to the year 2015, where skateboards can fly and all of the streets are elevated. The firm of Industrial Light and Magic worked on the effects, which included a lot of miniatures of the buildings and highway. In one incredible sequence Fox not only plays his older self but also his own son and daughter. A motion-control split screen combined all three characters, played by the same actor, into one seamless shot.

The film engendered controversy when critics learned the ending was a cliffhanger and audiences would have to wait several months for yet another sequel to see how it all came out. There was also negative publicity when a stuntwoman was injured during one of the flying skateboard sequences.

All was forgiven when *Back to the Future 3* (1990) came out and delighted just about everyone. In this film, Lloyd has gone back in time to the Wild West. Fox has learned that Lloyd will not live happily ever after in his favorite time period, but is fated to die soon after arriving in the western community. Fox goes back in time to try to prevent this from happening.

The picture speediy proceeds to a climax that answers the questions: Will Lloyd and the schoolmarm have a long life together? Will Fox survive a gunfight with a villan who's challenged his bravery; and will the DeLorean time machine, pushed by a locomotive, manage to build up enough speed to zip into the future before it reaches the crumbled bridge spanning an overpass? While not a perfect movie, *Back to the Future 3* provides the answers in a very entertaining fashion.

Spielberg's film *Young Sherlock Holmes* (1985) was an interesting film that was a commercial failure. In the film, detective Holmes and Watson meet as young men at school. The two investigate when

a series of men are injected with a drug that caus-
es hallucinations.This leads to the discovery of a
secret cult that has an enormous headquarters under London. Fine special effects for the halluci-
nation sequences feature some wonderful stop-motion
work: food come to life, as does a knight from a
stained-glass window. Director Barry Levinson failed to inject the film with enough flair or suspense,
however.

Spielberg wrote the story for *The Goonies* (1985),
an awful movie about a group of kids looking for
treasure in an underground lagoon. There are many
jokes about a clumsy, overweight kid who con-
stantly talks about food—talk about cliches! Director Richard Donner wasn't pleased when producer Spielberg removed a sequence where the
kids are attacked by a giant octopus. The octopus
was thirty feet long and had an evil eye that was
nearly half-a-foot wide. The scene was cut, but a
line of dialogue referring to the octopus was left
in, oddly enough.

Said one critic: "[Screenwriter] Chris Columbus
pays too much attention to cartoon violence and not
enough to characterization The kids aren't all that
different from one another."

Batteries Not Included (1987) was the story of
tiny flying saucers with distinct personalities who

interact with the tenants of a rundown city building. These saucers can even give birth to baby saucers! The saucers were ten inches in diameter and could be plugged into electric outlets. Most of their movements were the product of stop-motion, go-motion, and other processes. Sometimes simple puppetry, a hand inside the saucer, was employed. the script had been written for Spielberg's television series, *Amazing Stories*. Most people believed it never should have been made into a full-length movie.

Who Framed Roger Rabbit?(1988) was better received by audiences and critics. In this blend of cartoon animation and live-action, a private detective is hired to find out who is framing the title character, a goofy cartoon rabbit, for the murder of a human being. Virtually every cartoon character from any and all studios makes a guest appearance. The human protagonist winds up in a cartoon dimension where the usual laws of science do not apply (which is always the case in cartoons).

The film was co-produced by Spielberg's and Walt Disney's production studios. Executives at Disney were thunderstruck when Spielberg decided not to use their animators for the cartoon work. Instead, Spielberg and director Robert Zemeckis used a London animator named Richard Williams.

He eventually wound up using several Disney employees to help him with all the work.

The actors first rehearsed their scenes with life-size cardboard cut-outs or human stand-ins substituting for the cartoon characters,who were added much later. When the actors were certain of the motions they needed to make, the cut-outs and stand-ins were removed and the scene was filmed. The cartoon characters were inserted into the live action. The result was a very clever and amusing story of the cartoon characters, or "toons," trying to save their beloved "toon town" from an evil renegade "toon" who wants to destroy them all. In some strange way the movie even managed to be touching.

Arachnophobia (1990) was a comedy thriller directed by Frank Marshall, who had co-produced many of the previous films with Spielberg. In this film, a small-town doctor is horrified to learn that an enormous South American spider (or arachnid) has taken up residence on his property and its babies are causing havoc all over town. For real spider-chills, the picture can't compare to the fifties' creature feature, *Tarantula*, which features a bug as big as a house and is a lot more entertaining.

Casper (1995) was a live-action film based on the old cartoons of a lovable little boy ghost who wants to make friends. Unfortunately, his spectral appearance only scares everyone off. The cartoons had a certain poignancy to them, but it was decided to make a radical change for the motion picture. Instead of being this rather sad figure, Casper became a wise-alecky punk with "attitude." Casper was the result of computer graphics. Director Brad Silberling worked closely with the lead animator for each sequence.

"I basically ran through a sequence with him, shot-for-shot, pose-for-pose, eyebrow-crunch-for-eyebrow-cruch, and direct him as to what I want to see on the screen," said Silberling. The animator would then work on an Amiga computer system and do a kind of "rough sketch." When these were approved, they were overlaid onto the live-action footage. A videotape of the scene was sent to the firm of Industrial Light and Magic who came up with the final shots.

Twister (1996) was about a group of tornado experts tracking the latest cyclone. Or rather, it was about the devastation that the twister leaves in its wake. Startling FX work even showed cows flying through the air. Again, computers were used to create some astonishing shots. The movie has an entertaining climax when the romantic leads are caught in the most violent rush of the tornado but somehow manage to survive.

Spielberg also co-produced *Twilight Zone—The Movie* (1983), which was based on the popular TV series. Spielberg and three other directors helmed one segment apiece. Spielberg's portion, "Kick the Can,"is the weakest of the four, but works the best because of the sensitive acting and direction. It's a heavy-handed yet touching tale of nursing home oldsters magically transformed into children. The rest of the movie is forgettable.

The picture got very negative publicity when actor Vic Morrow and two small children were killed during a helicopter accident during filming., (This occurred during a segment directed by John Landis). Union rules prohibited the children from working on the set during the early morning hours when the tragedy took place. Landis was indicted for involutary manslaughter, but was acquitted.

Spielberg decided to produce his own *Twilight Zone*-type series for TV, *Amazing Stories*, in 1986. NBC gave him a terrific deal: he'd get one million dollars for each half-hour episode, and a guarantee that the show would run for two years before it could be cancelled. Creatively, the show was his baby, except having to account to the Broadcast Standards Department like everyone else did.

It wasn't long before NBC execs regretted the

deal. *Amazing Stories* was a stinker. For example, in one not-so-amazing story, a plain, chubby girl with braces has a crush on a good-looking but insensitive lad. Through idiotic circumstances, this lad turns into a human magnet. Guess who's literally attracted to him? The girl with the braces, who, because of her braces, can't pull away from him, even if she wanted to. The boy squirms. End of terrible story.

Not every story was so slight and silly, but even the "better" ones were minor to the extreme. The series plodded on for two seasons before being put out of its misery. Another Spielberg-produced TV show, a cartoon series called *Family Dog*, was also a big flop.

Spielberg decided he had better stick to making movies.

Chapter 8

Fantasy and Reality

'I'm very frustrated when I see (serious) movies," Spielberg has said. "I haven't taken a position personally on how I feel about the world. I think my films will eventually get around to that, but I never want to stop entertaining."

The fact was that, while Spielberg had made a lot of money, he had yet to convince many of his critics that he was a serious filmmaker. Despite—or perhaps because of—their undeniable entertainment allure, his movies were considered to be comparatively frivolous. It was a question as to whether or not he could craft a genuine work of art.

Spielberg wanted to satisfy his critics and prove he could do a fine job with a human story that did not rely on special effects, killer sharks, or aliens. Warner Brothers Studio owned the rights to a Pulitzer Prize-winning novel entitled *The Color Purple* by Alice Walker. It was the story of a black wo-

man in the South in the first half of the twentieth
century and how she triumphs over oppression and
adversity. The title comes from the line: "It pisses
God off if you walk by the color purple in a field
and don't notice it."

Celie (Whoopie Goldberg) is hideously exploit-
ed by her father, and sold to a husband, Albert, who
treats her miserably. The only thing that keeps her
going is the hope of being reunited with her sister Nettie, who has become a missionary in Africa.
Ironically, Celie's relationship with Shug, the woman that her husband is really in love with, gives
Celie some much-needed self-esteem.

Tongues wagged in Hollywood when it was
revealed that Spielberg was going to direct the film
adaptation of Walker's novel. Few thought he was
capable of dealing with this very personal, sensitive drama that featured both black and gay characters and was miles away from Spielberg's own
persona. Others felt that because Spielberg himself
belonged to a minority, he would relate to these
characters better than people anticipated.

Spielberg certainly related to the movie's star,
Whoopie Goldberg. The two became friends and
worked extremely well together. Whoopie is very
good, but Desreta Jackson, who plays the same
character as a girl, is truly outstanding. As Sophia,

Celie's daughter-in-law, Oprah Winfrey radiates the authority and aggressiveness that turned her into a talk show superstar and billionairess.

The Color Purple is well-directed by Spielberg. The cinematography and period settings are excellent. Spielberg had plenty of time to work with the actors, now that there were no big action scenes or FX to deal with. Outstanding scenes include the one where Albert throws Nettie off his property as a tortured Celie begs her to stay; Shug singing a song to Celie as she smiles in shy appreciation; and the touching end when the two sisters and their children are finally reunited.

Although the film won many respectful reviews, there were also charges that Spielberg had watered down and altered the book to reflect his world view. There are several instances where inappropriate comic relief was inserted to increase mass audience appeal. These include a cliched "funny" bar fight scene that gives the picture an old-fashioned quality. At the end of the film, Shug leads a whole group of people into the church where her estranged father is preaching and the two miraculously reunite. The scene is lively but also pat and contrived, like a TV sit-com.

In addition, there are so many characters and the film covers so many years, that it often gets confusing. Some scenes don't make sense, scenes in which the characters' actions aren't consistent. It was as if Spielberg was determined to wrap everything up in a "sunshine and light" finale that has little to do with reality—or the novel. Said one critic: "It was such a cartoon. He took this wonderful material and turned it into a zip-a-dee-doo-dah *Song of the South*."

Despite this criticism, the film received eleven Academy Award nominations. (It lost all of them.) Spielberg was not even nominated, but he did win a Best Director award from the Director's Guild, a prestigious consolation prize. Once again one of his movies made lots of money. *The Color Purple* cost $15 million and brought in $142 million at the box office.Whatever its flaws, T*he Color Purple* is a good picture if not a truly great one.

The same could be said of Speilberg's next "serious" picture, *Empire of the Sun* (1987)—although Spielberg took a step backwards with this one. The film takes place in Shanghai in 1941 during the Japanese war in China. As one British family joins the evacuation, twelve-year-old Jamey is separated from his parents. The film details his adventures, from his point of view, as he endures imprisonment in a prisoner of war camp.

The film has lots of interesting detail and

atmosphere, and the production is excellent on all levels—photography, editing, and Spielberg's direction. There are many good scenes, such as when the boy's young Japanese friend is killed, and his moving reunion with his parents at the finale. The boy's view of the city as he rides in a chauffeured car early in the picture, so detached from everything he sees, is also interesting.

But the film's fatal flaw is that the central character of the boy is not that interesting. He never seems that concerned about either his situation or his parents. In trying to keep the film from being too "terrible" to take, Spielberg gave it the mindset of a Disney movie. It's all just a grand romp, as if it's just another adventure of, say, the Hardy Boys. Not only is the story stripped of much of its power by this approach, but the film is even rather boring at times.

Although Spielberg's contract ensured that he would make money off the film, *Empire of the Sun* did not make a profit for the studio and was not well received by the critics or public. It was loud, big, and splashy—with hundreds of extras— but there were no aliens, spaceships or killer sharks.

Spielberg's next film, a combination of the serious and the supernatural, was a romantic fantasy entitled *Always* (1989). It was an updated remake of a 1944 film entitled *A Guy Named Joe*. Steven saw it for the first time on television when he was fourteen years old and it moved him to tears. He had always dreamed of doing his own version of it when the time was right. The influence of *A Guy named Joe* could be seen in some of his early movies, particularly in the relationships between the male and female leads.

Filled with improbabilities and dated period references, *A Guy Named Joe* has not held up very well over the years. Unfortunately, Spielberg's remake isn't much better. In fact, it's probably the most boring picture he has ever made.

The story has to do with a firefighter (Richard Dreyfuss) who is killed in an accident. He returns to earth to say good-bye to his girlfriend (Holly Hunter) and to help her go on with her life. Working behind the scenes (he is a ghost, after all), he helps in her love affair with another firefighter.

There are some good scenes in *Always*, and exciting aerial footage and forest fires that are expertly muddled and confused. In one, Holly Hunter, also a firefighter, crash-lands in water. Still grieving over Dreyfuss, she makes no move to save herself, Instead, Dreyfuss' spirit goes down to her plane and somehow pulls her from the water.

The film early established that it was necessary

for Hunter to decide on her own to go on with her life without Dreyfuss. We can't blame Dreyfuss for saving her, but it negates the idea that Hunter will be okay without Dreyfuss. Particularly when it was only Dreyfuss' spirit, her memories of and love for him, that got her out of the plane. Spielberg seems to be saying that Hunter is ready to move on to a new relationship. Clearly that is not the case.

Tedious rather than touching, *Always* only proved that, no matter how talented, a director can be defeated by a bad script. All the FX and action and exciting stunts in the world can't make something out of nothing. Incredibly, *Always* still made money (although not on the level of Spielberg's mega-hits), but few people really enjoyed it.

In 1990, Spielberg hired Mike Ovitz, then chairman of Creative Artists Agency to be his agent. It was thought that big things were in the air, as clients of the powerful CAA are generally brought together with other CAA clients—actors, screenwriters and directors— for some high-octane productions. At the time of Speilberg's signing with CAA, a film entitled *Hook* was already in pre-production. When Spielberg expressed an interest in directing *Hook* himself, the original director was fired and paid off.

Hook answered the question: What happened to

Peter Pan when he grew up? It was a question that should never have been asked, not only because the film that was to emerge was so terrible. James M. Barrie, the playwright who created Peter Pan, clearly intended that his character would never grow up, so what was the point in making a film in which he did? In *Hook*, Peter has become a corporate attorney named Peter Banning (Robin Williams). He has a wife and children. Banning/Peter returns to Neverland when his children are kidnapped by the evil Captain Hook (Dustin Hoffman). In keeping with the times, the Lost Boys are now a multi-cultural bunch. After a lot of tiresome escapades, Hook is engulfed in the mouth of a huge crocodile statue that falls on top of him. Neverland is saved. Like *Always*, *Hook* is a good-looking picture that desperately needs a better script.

Admittedly, there are good scenes in the picture. These include Peter's flashbacks to his lost, pre-Neverland childhood and the scene when he learns to fly again. Robin Williams does well as Peter, but Hoffman (Hook), Maggie Smith (elderly Wendy), and Julia Robers (Tinkerbelle) are the cast standouts. Roberts gets across her hero-worship of and crush on Peter tellingly. Bob Hoskins and Charlie Korsmo are also fine as, respectivly, Hook's assistant, Smee, and Peter's young son.

The sets for *Hook* were gigantic, taking up nine soundstages on the Metro-Goldwyn-Mayer backlot. The pirate ship was eight feet long and so tall that the cinematographer had trouble getting the whole thing in one frame. When the ship was finished, the entire soundstage was flooded so the thing could float. The tree house set was also enormous, spilling out of one soundstage and into another.

Oddly enough, the boyish Spielberg did not like working with so many child actors at the same time. For one thing, he disliked being the mean old authority figure to the children. Once, he lost his temper because they were talking instead of listening to his directions. Spielberg loves children; but he didn't like to direct a bunch of them.

Hook was almost universally panned by the critics. But that didn't stop people from going to the film. *Hook* cost $60 million and earned $228 million.

Hardly a bomb.

Chapter 9

Holocaust and Heritage

The reaction to Spielberg's "serious" films had always been mixed, perhaps because he couldn't relate personally to them. Whatever its universal message of oppression, the lives of *The Color Purple* characters were far removed from his own. The same could cetainly be said of *Empire of the Sun*. *Always*, a semi-serious picture, may have been based on a movie that had made him cry, but it had nothing to do with Spielberg's own life.

As a boy, Spielberg had had mixed emotions about his being Jewish faith. In one Phoenix neighborhood in which he spent a few years, there were few Jewish families. Steven, in his own words, was "looking to assimilate." He did not like being a Jewish boy; it made him seem different from other children. At least this is what he told himself.

His grandfather was Orthodox, and would usually call Steven by his Hebrew name. Steven dreaded it when his grandfather opened the door of their house and call for him by this name in front of his friends when it was time for dinner.

Steven's ambivalence about being Jewish—being different—were apparent in his films. He was criticized for making two pictures in which the villains were cartoon Nazis. *Raiders of the Lost Ark* and *Indiana Jones and the Lost Crusade* failed to show the true evil of the Nazis, nor even mentioned their anti-semitism. Young people would never realize that those comical "goosesteppers" had been responsible for the deaths of millions of Jews and other "undesirables" in Nazi concentration camps.

Spielberg's feelings began to change when his grandparents "began dying and weren't in my life anymore." He realized that he was proud of and wanted to explore his Jewish heritage. His second wife, Kate Capshaw, converted to Judiasm. The Spielbergs' home is not a kosher one (in which Jewish religous laws are kept), but they do observe Jewish holidays. Spielberg plans to tell his own children about the Holocaust when they are older.

Or perhaps he'll just show them his finest film, *Schindler's List* (1993). Finally, Spielberg got the acclaim he always wanted. At last ,he made a film that was personal and meant something to him.

Schindler's List is the story of Oskar Schindler, a manufacturer who takes over a Polish factory that was taken from its original owner by the invading Nazis. Initially, Schindler is a Nazi, but as he learns of German atrocities, he becomes concerned for his Jewish workers. He keeps them out of death camps by arguing that they are "essential workers." But the workers are only making pots that are not essential to the war effort. Schindler uses all of his influence and money to save 1100 Jews from the gas chambers, literally buying many from the Nazis.

There is no denying that *Schindler's List* is a powerful and absorbing film—well-directed by Spielberg—but it just misses being truly great. The major flaw is that the characters aren't very well developed. We never learn much about Schindler, and the Jewish characters are all one-dimensional. Schindler's turning point— when he begins to feel guilt and sympathy for his workers— is not shown. Scenes that might have shown the personal lives of victims are lessened because the audience knows little about the people involved.

Some critics said a billionaire filmmaker born after World War II and who did not experience that period's horrors, could hardly identify with the concentration camp survivors in any real fashion.

In spite of this criticism, there are compelling scenes in the film, some of which are almost unbearable to see. These include the slaughter of

Jewish residents in the Warsaw ghetto; and a sequence when the children of Schindler's factory workers are taken away in trucks as the mothers are temporarily diverted. When they realize what's happened, they run after the trucks, screaming, desperate to have their children back.

Another poignant moment occurs when a small boy looks for a place to hide from the Nazis. Desperate, he jumps into a latrine in which some other children are already hiding. They tell him to leave, but he has no place to go. His lost expression, as he stands up to his armpits in liquid filth, is heartbreaking. We never learn of his ultimate fate, but undoubtedly it was not a happy one.

The powerful finale of a sobbing, guilt-wracked Schindler wishing he could have saved more of the Jewish workers. "That car could have paid for ten people," he cries, pointing to his expensive vehicle. *Schindler's List* illustrates the shallowness of having money without the maturity to use it responsibly.

Schindler's List made a profit of $73 million. It also won seven Oscars, including Best Picture and Best Director. But Spielberg doesn't consider the film his best work. In his opinion, a $60 million project called *Survivors of the Shoah* (the Hebrew word for the Holocaust) is his crowning achievement. With a staff of seventy-five, and hundreds of volunteers around the world, it is, according to Steven, "the largest visual archive of its kind ever."

Survivors of the Shoah is a collection of video-taped testimonies of Holocaust survivors. 300 people a week were inteviewed in front of video cameras. There are also maps, biograpical information, pictures of lost relatives, all of it on-line and accessed on a computer screen.

"I think it is a rescue mission," says Spielberg. "We're rescuing history, we're rescuing the future, and we have very few years to do it because these people are an average age of seventy-five. In twenty years, (they) are not going to be around anyore, but we'll have their stories. Like film, they will live forever."

Eventually, the Survivors of the Shoah Visual History Foundation will expand its video archives to include testimonies by individuals who belong to other groups persecuted by the Nazis, i.e., gay people and gypsies. The archives can also be used by Holocaust survivors to locate friends and relatives whose ultimate fate has been unknown to them for decades.

Spielberg has commented that the "ethnic cleansing" of Bosnia proves that the horrors of the Holocaust should never be forgotten.

Chapter 10

Dinosaurs!

People have always been fascinated by the concept of dinosaurs being alive in the 20th century. In 1864 French writer Jules Verne penned *A Journey to the Center of the Earth*, a tale of three men who descend into the deepest recesses of the earth. At one point, the men encounter gigantic prehistoric animals that have survived through the centuries In 1912 Sir Arthur Conan Doyle wrote a novel entitled, *The Lost World*. In his book, adventurers discover such creatures on a plateau in South America.

More recently, Harry Adam Knight wrote a book entitled, *Carnosaur* (1984). This tale brought dinosaurs into the modern world by presenting a private zoo filled with dinosaurs cloned from ancient cells. Author Michael Crichton took a similar idea and wrote a bestseller from it. In *Jurassic Park*, dinosaurs are cloned from blood cells found in prehistoric mosquitoes. They are to be exhibited in a public zoo on an island, but greed and unfortunate circumstances combine to make the experience a nightmare for the human inhabitants.

In Crichton's sequel, *The Lost World*, (without ever crediting the influence of Sir Arthur Conan Doyle), there is another island on which the animals in *Jurassic Park* were incubated. The full-grown animals have taken over the island and cause no shortage of problems for the motley crew of adventurers who have come there for various reasons.

When *Jurassic Park* (1993) became the top-grossing film in history, there was no doubt that he would direct the sequel, *The Lost World* (1997). Both films use state-of-the-art computer technology to bring the dinosaurs to life. In addition, some of the monsters are mechanized models.

Spielberg originally wanted huge robots to play the dinosaurs, a technique that didn't work in such films as *The Land That Time Forgot* (1975). He also toyed with the idea of using stop-motion and go-motion puppets. But these techniques would require the use of many "process shots" in which monsters and people would be on separate pieces of film and have to be combined. Spielberg preferred an approach that would make it look as if the characters and the dinosaurs were actually in the same shot together, simulating live action. But without real dinosaurs, how could he do it?

The answer was CGI, or Computer-Generated Imagery. Stop-motion experts were hired, but they had to learn to use a computer to work their magic with a computer rather than miniatures. They were surprised that the processes weren't as different as they thought. With computers, they could make the dinosaurs move as they wanted them to, make their skin wrinkle similar to a real animal's would, and place them in the same frame as the actors in a seamless fashion.

According to co-visual effects supervisor, Mark A. Z. Dippe, "Stop or go-motion puppets have very restricted movements because the puppets have to be supported by a physical rig. It's almost impossible to get the dinosaurs to fall down and roll over. In the computer world, there is total freedom of movement, and it's possible to simulate all the attributes of a living dinosaur, like muscle and bone and skin, and sweat and blood, which we can't do very well with a latex creature."

Spielberg still used a robot for most shots of the Tyrannosaurus Rex. This remote-controlled "animatronic" creature, while not as big as a real T-Rex, was eighteen feet tall and weighed several tons. In *Jurassic Park* this robot was used in the sequence when the T-Rex breaks out of confinement and attacks a jeep, particularly when only part of the creature is seen. Full-length shots of the T-Rex were done by computer. The ill Triceratops lying down was a detailed, full-scale prop with air-filled bladders inside, which made it "breathe.". Live-action dinosaurs were done by Stan Winston.The man responsible for the computer-generated, or "full motion," dinosaurs was Dennis Muren.

The FX people on *Jurassic Park* believed one scene in Crichton's novel, when the T-Rex picks up a jeep with its teeth, was implausible. Instead, they have the animal push the jeep with its head. In his sequel, Crichton got back at the movie people by ridiculing an idea, introduced in the movie but was not in his novel. The film suggests that if a person were to stand perfectly still, the T-Rex could not find him. In *The Lost World* Crichton reminds everyone that the T-Rex would not have to see someone to eat him; it would only have to use its sense of smell! (In a scene in Jurassic Park, the T-Rex is clearly seen sniffing human star Sam Neill).

In *Jurrassic Park* , there is one sequence that raised a few eyebrows. This is when the T-Rex attacks one of the jeeps riding through the park and terrorizes the young boy and girl inside the car. The adults in a nearby jeep seem to take forever to attempt a rescue.The scene borders on the sadistic as far as the children are concerned, yet the same people who protested the allegedly gruesome heart-tearing in *Indiana Jones and the Temple of Doom* were apparently unbothered by it. The T-Rex biting a man in half is another grisly touch.

The film is filled with amazing scenes, as when the T-Rex chases after a jeep and nearly catches up wth it. The first view of the gigantic four-legged Brachiosauri stretching their long necks up to eat leaves is wondrous and majestic. And the scene of scientist Neill and the small boy frantically trying to climb down a tree before a car in the branches can fall on them is very exciting. But one has to wonder: Why didn't they climb up the tree and out of danger instead?

The human characters are better developed than in most Spielberg special effects extravagan-zas. As the picture proceeds, Neill, who doesn't want any children, begins to bond with the small boy and his older sister.

Jurassic Park and *The Lost World* are entertaining movies with great special effects. But as dinosaur classics go, they may be a bit behind the decades-old masterpiece *King Kong* (1933). That film may have old-fashioned FX work, but it's still grand entertainment with nary a dull stretch. Spielberg's dino-flicks get a trifle boring while the audience is waiting for the next big dinosaur to come along. Another problem is they create a sense of wonder over the special effects technology bringing the dionsaurs to life, but little over dinosaurs them-selves. People go on about the extinction of the dinosaurs, but Spielberg's movies never talk about how they dominated the earth for over 150 million years. Human beings have been around for just a small micro-fraction of that time.

Dinosaurs were actually a fascinating success story!

So was *Jurassic Park,* which grossed $850 mil-lion. *The Lost World* was expected to do as well, if not better.

Epilogue

Steven Spielberg the filmmaker represents both the best and worst of Hollywood, just as Steven Spielberg the man combines both positive and negative attributes. Steven didn't sit around dreaming about great things he could do; he took the initiative and went out and made it happen. Where some people are content to shrug and think "that will never happen to me, " Spielberg made his student movies, patronized contacts at the movie studios, and literally barreled his way into the industry that he wanted to be a part of.

No one may ever have heard of Steven Spielberg if he hadn't done this, but one can't help but think that perhaps somewhere out there are talented filmmakers who never got a chance because their approach wasn't quite so aggressive. His success, therefore, offers parallel messages: a) doers, not dreamers, are more likely to succeed; and b) success is not always relative to talent. The biggest is not always the best.

This is not to say that Spielberg is untalented,

which is not true. His drive and energy and persistence can also not be underestimated. Of course, what would have happened had *Jaws* not been such a runaway success? What if he hadn't convinced the producers to give him the assignment? Sometimes success and failure can hinge on things that the individual has no control over. Spielberg may have made millions of dollars many times over, but this doesn't automatically make him the finest filmmaker who ever lived. His work must be looked at objectively without regard to its commercial success.

How does Spielberg represent both the best and worst aspects of the film industry? His best films are full of cinematic energy, solid craftsmanship, and good old-fashioned entertainment values side-by-side with state-of-the-art technology. Have dinosaurs ever seemed more alive than in *The Lost World*? On the other hand, his films rely too much on special effects and not enough on human values. Even his serious films, such as *The Color Purple* and *Schindler's List* aren't as great as they could have been.

The Lost World summarizes Spielberg's strengths and weaknesses, particularly the scene when the two T-Rexes knock the van off the cliff. Two of the characters—Jeff Goldblum's girlfriend and another man played by Vince Vaughn—inadvertently attract the grown T-Rex because they have stupidly brought the injured T-Rex offspring into the van. The sequence is gut-wrenching and suspenseful, the dinosaurs look uncomfortably realistic, and the audience is on the edge of its seat. The man who risks his own life to try to save the people in the van is torn in half and devoured by the T-Rexes.

Afterward, Jeff Goldblum berates another character for appearing callous about this man's death—the film's only moment of humanism—but Vaughn and the woman have absolutely no reaction! Their friend and co-worker died saving their lives because of their own stupidity, and they seem totally unaffected by it.

Perhaps these two characters were meant to be seen as cold-blooded creeps, but the movie never deals with it, too busy with dino-mayhem to bother. *The Lost World* thrills, but a really great picture would not mindlessly gloss over the incident, and a truly great director would never allow such bad, unemotional acting. It's almost as if Spielberg were saying: "This will be a big film , it will gross 100 million. It's only about dinosaurs, so who cares? Besides, didn't I have enough 'humanity' in *Schindler's List*?" Regardless of the genre, the thing that separates a good picture from schlock isn't the special effects, but the treatment of its characters.

Like too many in the motion picture and television industry, Spielberg is not much of a reader. Characters can be explored more fully in books, and literate screenwriters are more likely to create cinematic counterparts that live and breathe instead of just saying their lines. Spielberg doesn't seem to have the gift of other directors (like Alfred Hitchcock) to take a weak screenplay and fix it before shooting begins. He does not read (much), he cannot write (well), and his films suffer because of it.

Spielberg's determination to be ranked among the greatest "serious" filmmakers can be seen from his choice of subject matter in his most recent pictures. He was disappointed by the critical and (comparative) financial failure of *Amistad*, a film that examined the plight of African slaves brought to the New World. Although he was given an "A" for intentions, critics carped about the oversimplification of serious issues and the one-dimentsional nature of the characters. The general feeling was that the subject matter deserved—cried out for—better treatment.

But Steven was vindicated with his very next release, Saving Private Ryan, starring Tom Hanks. In this powerful World War Two film, Hanks leads a squad of G.I.s on D-Day to find a soldier, Private Ryan, whose three brothers have already been killed. Once they find him, Ryan is to be sent back to the United States to avoid being killed as well. The critical consensus was that Spielberg had directed a bonafide masterpiece, and veterans of that great conflict came forward to say that this was the first time a movie had shown what it was really like to be a soldier in the midst of a terrible, bloody battle. The graphic, indeed gruesome, combat sequences were unsparing in their intensity. While these scenes were, understandably, very disturbing to many viewers, Spielberg felt this approach was necessary to make it clear that war was really Hell. It is expected that *Saving Private Ryan* will sweep the Oscars.

Anyone who has sat through *Indiana Jones and the Temple of Doom, Jaws, Close Encounters* and *Jurassic Park*, or was moved by *Schindler's List, The Color Purple* or *Saving Private Ryan*—and they are legion—can testify that whatever his flaws as a filmmaker, Steven Spielberg has entertained and enlightened billions of people. In particular, with *Schindler's List* he reminded the world—a world in which some people try to say the holocaust never happened—that we musn't forget the past and the lessons we can learn from it.

And that's not a bad legacy for anyone.

Filmography

Sugarland Express (1974)
Jaws (1975)
Close Encounters of the Third Kind (1970
1941 (1979)
Raiders of the Lost Ark (1981
ET: The Extraterrestrial (1982)
Twilight Zone: The Movie (1983)
Indiana Jones and the Temple of Doom (1984)
Color Purple (1985)
Empire of the Sun (1987)
Indiana Jones and the Lost Crusade (1989)
Always (1989)
Hook (1991)
Jurassic Park (1993)
Schindler's List (1995)
Lost World (1996)

Producer/Co-Producer/Co-Author

I Wanna Hold Your Hand (1978)
Used Cars (1980)
Continental Divide (1981)
Poltergeist (1982)
Twilight Zone—The Movie (1983)
Gremlins (1984)
Back to the Future (1985)
The Goonies (1985)
Young Sherlock Homes (1985)
The Money Pit (1986)
*Batteries Not Included (1987)

Innerspace (1987)
Back to the Future II (1989)
Dad (1989)
Back to the Future III (1990)
Joe Versus the Volcano (1990)
Arachnophobia (1990)
Gremlins 2: The New Batch (1990)
The Flintstones (1994—as Steven Spielrock)

Animated Films

An American Tail (1986)
The Land Before Time (1988)
Who Framed Roger Rabbit? (1988) (combined live actiion
    and animation)
An American Tail: Fievel Goes West (1991)
We're Back! A Dinosaur (1993)

Television

Night Gallery (segments of telefilm, 1969)
Duel (1971)
Something Evil (1972)
Savage (1973)
"The Toon Adventures" (series, 1990-   )
"Family Dog" (1993)
"Animaniacs" (1993—   )
"Amazing Stories" (1985-87)
"The Water Engine" 1992)
"Class of '61" (telefilm)
"SeaQuest DSV" (series)

Awards

Nominated for Academy Award for Best Director (1977)
Close Encounters of the Third Kind

Irving G. Thalberg Award (1987)

Best Director/Best Picture (1995
Schindler's List

Bibliography

Bartholomew, David. "E. T." *Cinefantastique*. November/ December, 1982.

Gottleib, Carl. *The Jaws Log.* New York: Dell Publishing Company, 1975.

Harryhausen, Ray. *Film Fantasy Scrapbook.* New York: A. S. Barnes and Co., 1972.

Kaplan, Michael. E. T. and Me."*Cinefantastique,*September/ October, 1982.

Quirk, Lawrence J. *The Films of Joan Crawford.* Secaucus, N. J.: citadel Press, 1971.

Sanello, Frank. *Spielberg: The Man, The Movies, The Mythology.* Dallas: Taylor, 1996.

Schoel, William. *Stay Out of the Shower: Twenty-five Years of Schocker Films Beginning With "Psycho."* New York: December, 1985.

_____. "Things That Go Boom! in the Night." *The Scream Factory.* No. 8, 1991-1992.

20/20 (TV program), NBC television, October 20, 1994.

Van Hise, James. "Poltergeist." *Cinefantastique,* Vol. 13, nos. 2 and 3, 1982.

Villard, Robert and Dan Scapperotti. "Close Encounters of the Third Kind." *Cinefantastique*, Vol 6, no. 4, and Vol. 7, no. 1, 1978.

Index